La Famiglia
The Family

Lewis Turco

Bordighera Press

Library of Congress Control Number: 2009905032

Printed in the United States.

Published by
BORDIGHERA PRESS
John D. Calandra Italian American Institute
25 West 43rd Street, 17th Floor
New York, NY 10036

VIA FOLIOS 57
ISBN 978-1-59954-006-1

OTHER BOOKS BY LEWIS TURCO

Fiction and Poetry

The Museum of Ordinary People and Other Stories, 2008
Fearful Pleasures: The Complete Poems, 2007
The Collected Lyrics of Lewis Turco / Wesli Court, 2004
A Book of Fears, 1998
Emily Dickinson, Woman of Letters, 1993
The Shifting Web: New and Selected Poems, 1989
The Compleat Melancholick, 1985
American Still Lifes, 1981
Pocoangelini: A Fantography & Other Poems, 1971
The Inhabitant, 1970
Awaken, Bells Falling: Poems 1959–1967, 1968
First Poems, 1960

Nonfiction

Satan's Scourge: A Narrative of the Age of Witchcraft, 2009
Fantaseers, A Book of Memories, 2005
The Book of Dialogue, 2004
A Sheaf of Leaves, Literary Memoirs, 2004
The Book of Forms, A Handbook of Poetics, Third Edition, 2000
The Book of Literary Terms, 1999
Il Dialogo, Italian translation by Sylvia Biasi of *Dialogue*, 1992
Visions and Revisions of American Poetry, 1986

DEDICATION

For my little sweethearts
Jessima Ranney and Phoebe Norman
and my brother's little sweetheart and pals,
Ciara, Alex, Jack and Ryan Turco

ACKNOWLEDGMENTS

I wish to thank a great many people for their help and encouragement throughout my life, but in particular my wife, Jean, for far too many reasons to list here, but specifically for her labors during the academic year 1968–69 on my father's manuscript, *The Spiritual Autobiography of Luigi Turco,* which rests in the archives of the Center for Immigration Studies at the University of Minnesota whose original director, the late Rudolph J. Vecoli, requested my father's papers. It is that manuscript that provided much of the material herein contained.

I also want to thank all my family members for their input into this Italian-American book of memories, but especially my cousin Ann Buttigheri Badach, who we discovered is a born writer — would that we had known sooner! She has the best memory and the largest store of information of any of those of the older members of our clan who are left. She, my brother and I are all that remain of the second generation of immigrants from Riesi, Sicily.

I also owe a great debt of gratitude to all the editors and publishers who, over the past half-century and more, have midwived my work; a few of them are listed below for materials that appear herein:

"Cancer" was originally published in *The Sewanee Review* and collected in *Fearful Pleasures: The Complete Poems of Lewis Turco 1959–2007* (Scottsdale AZ: Star Cloud Press.com), © 2007 by Lewis Turco. It is reprinted here by permission of the author and the publisher.

"The Church" and "Failed Fathers" first appeared in *La Fusta.* The former was anthologized and reprinted with an Italian translation by Ferdinando Alfonsi in *Poeti Italo-Americani / Italo-American Poets,* edited by Ferdinando Alfonsi (Catanzaro, Italy: Antonio Carello Editore, 1985); the latter was anthologized in *Don't Tell Mama! The Penguin Book of Italian-American Writing,* edited by Regina Barreca (New York: Penguin, 2002). Both poems were collected in *Fearful Pleasures, op. cit.* They are reprinted here by permission of the author and the publisher.

"Conceit" first appeared in *VIA: Voices in Italian Americana* and was collected in *Fearful Pleasures, op. cit.* It is reprinted here by permission of the author and the publisher.

"Dawn Song" was first published in *The Laurel Review* and was gathered in *The Collected Lyrics of Lewis Turco / Wesli Court 1953–2004* (Scottsdale AZ: Star Cloud Press.com, © 2004 by Lewis Turco); by permission of the author and the publisher.

"Deep Ancestry," "A Letter to My Son" by Luigi Turco, and "Reunions" appeared on the Internet blog, *Poetics and Ruminations,* © 2007 by Lewis Turco.

"The Glass Cup" was published originally in *The Kansas Quarterly*; reprinted here by permission of the author.

"A Hollow Rush," which is contained in "A Letter to My Son" by Luigi Turco, was first published in *The Midwest Quarterly* and subsequently collected in *The Collected Lyrics, op. cit.* where it appears under the title, "It Goes." Reprinted here by permission of the author and the publisher.

"Hornpipe Epithalamium" and "The Lament of Turko the Terrible" were first published in *Song* 5 (1978), and gathered in *The Collected Lyrics, op. cit.* They appear here by permission of the author and the publisher.

"The Hustle," which first appeared in *Courses in Lambents* by Wesli Court (Oswego: Mathom, 1977), is reprinted here from *The Collected Lyrics, op. cit.*, by permission of the author and the publisher.

"An Immigrant Ballad" was included on the record album *Anthology of Contemporary American Poetry* edited and performed by George Abbe (New York: Folkways Records, 1961), and reprinted in *La Storia: Five Centuries of the Italian American Experience* by Jerre Mangione and Ben Morreale (New York: HarperPerennial, 1993). It was gathered in *The Collected Lyrics, op. cit.*

"A Letter to My Cousin Lewis" by Ann Badach Buttigheri, "Father and Son," and "'Little' Josephine" appeared originally in *VIA: Voices in Italian Americana* as did "Lemon Ice," which also appeared in the anthology *Two Worlds Walking,* edited by Diane Glancy and C. W. Truesdale (Minneapolis: New Rivers Press, 1994). Reprinted by permission of the authors.

The poem titled "A Medicine for Melancholy" was originally titled "To Smoke a Pipe" and appeared in *Voices* in 1962; it was collected under its current title in my book *The Compleat Melancholick* in 1985 and ultimately in *Fearful Pleasures, op. cit.*

"Mrs. Martino the Candy Store Lady" was first published in *The Beloit Poetry*

Journal in 1960, and collected in *Fearful Pleasures, op. cit.*

"The Mutable Past" appeared in *The Virginia Quarterly Review* in 1995 and was reprinted in *Fantaseers, A Book of Memories* (Scottsdale: Star Cloud Press, 2005).

"The Obsession" appeared originally in *New CollAge*; it was first anthologized in both *Patterns of Poetry,* edited by Miller Williams (Baton Rouge: Louisiana State UP, 1986), and *The New Book of Forms: A Handbook of Poetics* by Lewis Turco (Hanover NH: UP of New England, © 1986 & 2000); reprinted by permission of the publisher and the author.

"Pocoangelini XII," included in the review by Felix Stefanile of *Pocoangelini: A Fantography and Other Poems,* which appeared in *Italian Americana* (Spring 1975), is quoted here by permission.

"The Recurring Dream" first appeared in *The Hudson Review* and was collected in *Fearful Pleasures, op. cit.* Reprinted by permission of the author and the publisher.

"Requiem for a Name" was published originally in *The Carleton Miscellany* and gathered in *The Collected Lyrics, op. cit.* Reprinted by permission of the author and the publisher.

"Sandcastles" by Melora Turco Norman was published in *Lewis Turco and His Work: A Celebration,* edited by Dr. Steven E. Swerdfeger, PhD (Scottsdale AZ: Star Cloud Press.com, 2004); reprinted by permission of the author and the publisher.

"The Shambling Man" was first published in *The North Atlantic Review,* by permission of the author.

"The Story of an Italian Protestant" was first published in 2007 in *Italian Americana* of the University of Rhode Island at Providence. The poem/essay titled "Minotaur" was published in the same periodical in 1999; however, the poem itself first appeared in *NewCollage* of New College, Sarasota, Florida, in the 1975–76 issue, and it was reprinted in that periodical's 20th anniversary issue in 1989; it was reprinted again in *Poetry Pilot* of the Academy of American Poets in the Nov.-Dec. 1991 issue edited by Dana Gioia titled, "What Is Italian-American Poetry?" and a part of an autobiography, "Lewis Putnam Turco," in *Contemporary Authors Autobiography Series,* Vol. 22, edited by Joyce Nakamura for Gale Research, 1995. The poem alone was anthologized in *Wild Dreams: The Best of Italian Americana* edited by Carol Bonomo Albright and Joanna Clapps Herman for Fordham University Press, 2008, and it was first collected in a chapbook titled *A Maze of Monsters,* Livingston University Press, 1986, and most recently in

Fearful Pleasures, op. cit.

"Street Meeting" and the discussion of it by Stanley Romaine Hopper were first published in the anthology *Riverside Poetry 3,* edited by Marianne Moore, Howard Nemerov, and Alan Swallow (New York: Twayne, 1958). The poem was gathered in *The Collected Lyrics, op. cit.* Reprinted by permission of the author and the publisher.

"Upstairs" first appeared in *How We Work,* edited by Marla Morris, Mary Aswell Doll and William F. Pinar (New York: Peter Lang, 1999). Reprinted by permission of the author.

The discussion of "The View from a Winter Garret" is excerpted from "Periodical Parade, or, The Beat Goes On" by T. L. Ponick, editor of, and published in, *Edge City Review.* The poem was originally published in *Sparrow* 65 (September 2000), edited by Felix Stefanile.

"Vigilance" was first published in *Ploughshares* in 1979 and collected in *Fearful Pleasures, op. cit.*

An excerpt from "The House of Dreams" appeared as "The Bath" on-line in 2008, and "A Nest of Inlaws" was published on-line in 2009 in *Nights and Weekends*.com, and appears here by permission of the author and the publisher.

Versions of five of these memoirs — "Lemon Ice," "Gene and Genes," "Father and Son," "Jean," and "Mom May" — have previously appeared in a monograph, *Shaking the Family Tree,* published by Bordighera, Inc., and copyright © 1998 by Lewis Putnam Turco.

Lewis Turco
Dresden, Maine
21 August 2008

TABLE OF CONTENTS

UPSTAIRS: AN INTRODUCTION

On the theory that after more than four decades of marriage my wife Jean might possibly know more about how I work at my writing than I do, at least consciously, I asked her to help me with this essay. "When you're working," she said, "you're upstairs," meaning upstairs in my garret study in Oswego, New York, on blue Ontario's shores.

I waited for further information, but none was forthcoming. "That's it?"

She thought for a moment. She smiled. "When you come downstairs you're in a good mood." And that *is* it in a nutshell: writing makes me happy. I'm one of those people who enjoy writing, but to begin with, of course, I enjoyed reading.

In order to enjoy reading, however, one must be introduced to the practice. This is critically important, and one's early environment, I believe, is the key. Some people come to reading by accident, others are lucky to have parents who read, and often one's cultural heritage is either a help or a hindrance. In an essay titled "In Search of Italian / American Writers" Fred Gardaphé wrote the following:

> There were no bookshelves in my home. Reading anything beyond newspapers and the mail required escaping from my family. I soon developed a chronic reading problem that identified me as the "merican" or rebel. My reading betrayed my willingness to enter mainstream American culture, and while my family tolerated this, they did little to make that move an easy one.

Prof. Gardaphé came to reading circuitously:

> Once, while I was being chased by the police for disturbing local merchants so my partners could shoplift, I ran into the public library. I found myself in the juvenile section and grabbed a book to hide my face. Safe from the streets, I spent the rest of the afternoon reading, believing that nobody would ever find me there. And I was right, so whenever I was being chased, I would head straight for the library, which became my asylum.[1]

---

[1] Gardaphé, Fred, "In Search of Italian / American Writers," *Italian Americana* 2.1 (March 1997): 6.

Nothing could have been further from my own experience; however, thinking back on my early life, I consider it remarkable that my own parents, given their individual histories — impoverished childhoods in Sicily and Wisconsin, my mother a product of rural American penury, my father someone who wanted to be "someone," the only evident way to that goal being to join the local Mafia, a course he contemplated for a time — brought up their children as members of the middle class who had no doubt at all we were as privileged as anyone else. Thus, *attitude* is important, how one regards oneself, no matter what one's background may be.

Somehow, without what we now call a "role model," unless it was one or more of her teachers, my mother had managed to pull herself out of her parents' Superior, Wisconsin, shack, and work her way, first, through secretarial school and then through Boston University's School of Religious Education. Likewise, my father had extricated himself from Riesi, Sicily, and all sorts of menial jobs, to become pastor of the First Italian Baptist Church of Meriden, Connecticut.

Though we had no money, our house was full of books of all sorts. My mother read to me from the cradle, and I soon learned to read for myself. Nor was writing an abstruse act, because every week for as long as I can remember I watched my father hunched over his typewriter hunting out and pecking at his two weekly sermons, one in English and one in Italian.

From an early age, also, I was aware that my mother's family had a long and fascinating, if not always distinguished, history. George Puttenham, back in the sixteenth century, had been the author of *The Arte of English Poesie,* a fact that was fraught with omens for me, omens of which I was not completely aware when in 1959 I began writing my own *The Book of Forms: A Handbook of Poetics,* published first by E. P. Dutton in 1968. I knew, too, that Israel Putnam had been a general in Washington's colonial army and that Amelia Earhart had been married to George Palmer Putnam, the publisher. There have been many writers, librarians and teachers among the Putnams (my daughter, Melora, is a librarian), but there had been lots of farmers and artisans as well (my brother is a retired toolmaker).

In retrospect I can see that I was subjected to anti-Italian prejudice, even on the part of at least one of my teachers, but either I did not recognize it or I ignored or disdained it, for I always felt myself to be seminally involved with English and American literature because of my family connections with the majority culture. Felix Stefanile, reviewing *Pocoangelini, A Fantography & Other Poems* (1971) said,

"Turco seems to have the whole of the English lyric tradition at his fingertips. . . ."[2] That's because I have studied it closely all my life, taught it for more than three decades, and written out of it perfectly "naturally."

This business of prejudice is not uncomplicated. The title of my entry, during my senior high school year, in the school's Hicks Prize Essay Contest — one of the six finalists — was "A Row of Hedges," and it made an elaborate metaphor: the hedges outside the English Honors classroom, taught by Mark Bollman, represented the succession of our school years; the window cut off the view of the downhill end of the hedges, which represented the future, etc., etc. Quite corny, but decently written for a high school senior, evidently. I was told by other teachers that two of the three faculty judges thought my essay was the best one submitted that year, but that one judge, my English Honors teacher, refused to support it for the prize. In 1993 our old music teacher, Antonio Parisi, confirmed what I had long suspected: "Bollman hated Italians," he said. "You never stood a chance."

At Fenn College (now the Cleveland State University) at the beginning of my second year of teaching in 1961, I was asked to address the incoming students at the fall Freshman Convocation. Reaching back into my not-so-distant past, I refurbished "A Row of Hedges" and turned it into an exemplary talk about the importance of writing in college. Afterward one of the freshmen approached me to say, "I hope you don't expect us to write as well as that!" I didn't, but I wished I could have done so.

One supposes that teachers ought at least to try to be evenhanded with all their students and to recognize and reward merit no matter where it arises, but there is prejudice toward Italians even among members of the Italian-American community itself. Some of my father's Italian parishioners were unhappy because they had a "Sicilian" pastor, a standard distinction and bias, for Sicily is considered by Italians to the north to be ethnically part of Africa. And one can perhaps also imagine what the Italian Roman Catholics thought — they called my brother and me "the priest's kids".

Most of our parishioners lived in the neighborhood of the church, like the Poles who lived on Polish Hill near St. Stanislaus church. The Irish had their section of the city, as did the Germans, but none of the "ethnic" families that I knew wanted their children to be "Italian-Americans" or whatever-"Americans." They

---

[2]Stefanile, Felix, *Italian Americana* 1.2 (Spring 1975).

wanted them to be "Americans." The sooner into the melting pot, the better. My view of my "Italianness" has always been much closer to that of my old friend and mentor, the late John Ciardi, than it is to that of Gardaphé.

Vince Clemente, in an essay titled "The Writer as Hyphenated-American," wrote, "The critic Harold Bloom once came down heavily on the poet Stanley Kunitz for 'evading his Jewish heritage' in his poetry. Kunitz thought about that for a long time, and in his response articulated perfectly the plight of those American writers who carry with them, along with the burden to recreate the truth as they see it, the freight of ethnicity, this 'dual citizenship.' In a spring 1982 *Paris Review* interview Kunitz remarked:

> It's obvious that Jewish cultural aspiration and ethical doctrine entered into my bloodstream, but in practice I am an American free-thinker, a damn stubborn one, and my poetry is not hyphenated. . . . True, I have no religion, but I have strong religious feelings. Moses and Jesus and Lao-tse have all instructed me . . . and three of the poets who most strongly influenced me — Donne, Herbert, and Hopkins — happen to have been Christian churchmen."

Clemente continued, "The American poet and translator of Dante, John Ciardi, himself the son of Italian immigrant parents, wrote in an early letter to me, 'I have poured out endless poems about my Italian "roots." Yet Jefferson, Tom Paine, and even — God save the mark, Emerson — are as much at the roots of my mind and feeling as the It[alian] of my Am[erican]. I am an American man of letters!' Like Kunitz, Ciardi insisted his 'poetry is not hyphenated.' In fact, he once told me, 'In truth, my boyhood (in Boston's Little Italy and Medford, Massachusetts) was not so much an Italian-American one as *my* boyhood.' And just two weeks later, in another letter, he recalled, 'I had a longish poem about Italy in the *Atlantic* some years back, and when Robert Lowell wrote to praise its Italo-Amer[ican] voice, I took offense. Did the S.O.B. suppose I had used an Amer[ican] Eng[lish] inferior to his, or that I inherited and made mine less Amer[ican] Eng[lish] than his?'

"About that time," Clemente wrote, "I proposed to him the prospect of an anthology of 'Italian-American Poets.' He never really warmed up to the thing and wrote to the poet-critic Lewis Turco, 'I've never thought in terms of Italian-American poetry; I don't know any Italian-American poets, as such. Lew Turco is an American poet who happened to have [an Italian father]. Theodore Roethke is a ditto with German parents.' Now, all these years later," Clemente discovered, "I know just what Ciardi meant: Why isn't Archibald MacLeish a Scottish-American poet? Whitman, on his mother's side, a Dutch-American one? I like to feel the American experience is broad enough, indeed all-encompassing as Whitman's vision of it, to include all of us as simply 'Americans' without the hyphen."[3]

In a videotaped interview that he made for the "Writers' Forum" series at the SUNY College at Brockport (a tape I played about once a year for two decades in my contemporary American poetry class), Robert Hayden was asked about "Black poetry." His response was that such a term, which had the approval of many militant Black poets, was useful primarily to white academics who wish to ignore poetry written by blacks. The inference to be drawn therefrom, Hayden said, is that somehow poetry written by black Americans is not good enough, or not universal enough to be included in the Anglo-Saxon literary canon.[4]

In a letter dated February 24, 1976, Radcliffe Squires, in his capacity as editor of *The Michigan Quarterly Review*, published by the University of Michigan where Hayden was teaching at the time, wrote to one of his regular reviewers who happened to be a white academic — myself, to be specific, "to ask you if you could review Robert Hayden's *Angle of Ascent*. . . . He feels bad that every place seems to feel it must have him reviewed by another black. I agree that is both silly and intolerable. Anyway, I hope you will be willing to undertake this . . ." I was, and I did. (And since it appeared in *MQR* it has been anthologized several times.)

Hayden always wanted to be judged merely as a poet among poets, not one to whom special rules of criticism had to be applied in order to make his work acceptable in more than a sociological sense. His stance, reiterated in the Brockport interview, was well known for a long time both to militant blacks and to "liberal" whites. Thus, if the latter relegated Hayden to the literary ghetto along with the other Black poets, the former have seen him, if not as an "Uncle Tom," at least as a reluctant resident. Perhaps this situation best explains why Hayden was virtually ignored during his lifetime. Yet Hayden, like Ciardi, wrote as much out of his ethnicity as anyone else. He was a paradigmatic poet of the English language who was also true to his roots and history, though not circumscribed by what is merely racial, ethnic, or personal.

---

[3]Clemente, Vince, "The Writer as Hyphenated-American," *The Boston Book Review* (1996).
[4]Hayden, Robert, "The Poetry of Robert Hayden," *Writers' Forum* video archive, SUNY Brockport.

Just as Stanley Kunitz, John Ciardi, and Robert Hayden did, I sometimes write out of my ethnic "heritage." Writing in their book *La Storia: Five Centuries of the Italian American Experience,* Jerre Mangione and Ben Morreale said, "Not all of the immigrants' offspring who became poets were as much at ease in America as Ciardi. But the most gifted of them were able to transcend the specifics of the Italian American experience through the more subjective and symbolic language of their craft. For poets deeply imbued with the experience of trying to straddle two cultures, such as Lewis Turco and Frank Polite, poetry became the vehicle by which they could transmit the loneliness of their alienation with impunity, without denying or betraying their Italian connection."[5]

But I don't remember being alienated as an *Italian* American, though I certainly do as a *Protestant* Italian American. Mangione and Morreale continued, "Lewis Turco, one of the most prolific of the Italian American poets, gradually distanced himself from his past as he journeyed toward the mainstream. By the time he was in his thirties, in 1973, when he published *Pocoangelini: A Fantography,* Italianate poems constituted only a third of the contents."

Although it is true that I distanced myself from my youth, of course (everybody does), I never distanced myself from my ethnicity. I simply write poems and stories — and, of recent decades, essays and memoirs — as they occur to me, and if later on I feel that older material can be mined, transformed, or linked together to form longer works or sequences, so be it. That's what I have done in this book.

---

[5]Mangione, Jerre, and Ben Morreale, *La Storia, Five Centuries of the Italian American Experience* (New York: Harper, 1992) 430–34.

DAWN SONG

Many things fascinate me, but the idea of evolution fascinates me to the point of awe. One of the reasons I could not become the minister my pastor father wanted me to become is that I could not believe in a Creator, no matter how hard I tried. It didn't seem reasonable to me that a creature so great and complicated could have existed *a priori* and have invented the cosmos because all that does is beg the question, "Who (or What) created the Creator?" It is easier for me to believe that the cosmos forever existed, exists now, and will forever exist than it is to postulate an omnipotent Creator. He would have had to create Himself. That, in fact, may be what the Cosmos is doing: evolving the Godhead. I can at least experience through my senses elements of the cosmos.

If evolution is inventing a godlike creature, and if one of the avatars of that creature is mankind, then at some point in the history of that evolution one of the predecessors of mankind must have given birth to the first true human being. What would that have been like? One of the things I enjoy is reading anthropological works: I consider that Loren Eiseley's book *The Firmament of Time* is one of the great works of literature of the twentieth century, and another great writer of anthropology was Margaret Mead. Sometimes in my reading I come up against a passage that arrests my eyes and causes my mind to begin to spin a fable. Such a passage was this portion of a sentence by Mead: "*. . . world of the first rose, and the first lark's song.*"

What must it have been like for the first truly human being at dawn one day to awaken from her sleep, to look out on the savannah, and to realize that she was conscious of herself and of her plight and glory? To *know,* beyond all doubt, that she *knew*?

I am the first to know dawn for the dawn —
it breaks across my mind as across the eyes
of the beast I was, of the beasts from whom I come,
and the swift sun slows, and I know it for the sun
in the world of the first rose, and the first lark's song.

I am the first to see the sharp sun dawn,
breaking across my terror and my surprise;

to know that I am the beast who knows his name:
Beast of the Sun, beast of the spinning sun
of the world of the first rose, and the first lark's song.

I am the first to see stone for a stone,
to heft it in my hand, to feel its weight
and know what it may do to the brittle bone
of the beasts of the sun, in the morning of the sun,
in the world of the first rose, and the first lark's song.

I see, and my sight is hard, hard as the stone
held in my hand, and this stone will be my fate.
The beast is my brother — beast is his only name.
He is the child of dust. I am stone's son,
born of the first rose and the first lark's song.

DEEP ANCESTRY

Almost all my life I have known that my last name, Turco, in Italian means what it says: "Turk." It dates, I understand, from the period of the Arab rule of Sicily from the ninth to the tenth centuries, and it is not an uncommon name in Sicily where my father was born. Since there was no such place as Turkey at the time, the word simply means "Arab" or "Moor"; moreover, according to Halbert's,[1] a Turco family coat of arms can be found in *Rietstap Armorial General,* and the shield is described as "Silver with a Turk, facing front, dressed in a blue tunic and red pantaloons; wearing a red turban on his head, holding in his right hand a silver scroll, and in his left hand a silver scimitar trimmed gold. Family mottos are believed to have originated as battle cries in medieval times, but a motto was not recorded with the Turco coat of arms."

However, I am something of a cynic, and I have long believed in an adage that would serve well for any family's motto: "It is the wise child that knows its father." Since everyone has trampled over Sicily since time began, including Sicils, Greeks, Romans, Carthaginians, French, Vikings, Normans, Danes, English, and so on ad infinitum, many of them raping and pillaging as they wandered across the countryside, I assumed that somewhere along the line there must have been a break in the chain and that my name might as easily have been Smith or Jones as Turco. So when it became possible, I decided to have my DNA tested to see where I really came from.

In 2006 I participated in the National Geographic Human Genome Project[2] and discovered that my blood confirms what my name asserts: I am paternally a Turk through and through! Males are traced genetically through the Y-DNA marker which is passed down unchanged from father to son over generations; women are traced through their mothers' mitochondrial DNA which is passed from mother to daughter, also unchanged. Of course every now and then, at *great* intervals, both Y-DNA and mitochondrial DNA do take on characteristics that differentiate them from other evolutionary lines, and these mutated lines can be traced.

---

[1]"Turco Coat of Arms, Historiography," Bath, OH: Halberts, n.d.
[2]National Geographic Human Genome Project, www.NationalGeographic.com.

So far as can be discerned with the data currently at hand, it turns out that my father's branch of the Turco family is part of a group of people about which little is known. My Y-chromosome results identify us as members of haplogroup G, "a lineage defined," my National Geographic report stated, "by a genetic marker called M201" which had its origin some 60,000 years ago with an ancient Y-chromosome marker called M168.

According to Spencer Wells[3] there was a single male who lived perhaps 75,000–100,000 years ago whose mutated Y-chromosome is carried by every male currently alive. Although scientists call this person "Genetic Adam," or "Eurasian Adam," in fact he was not likely the first fully human male, but none of the other males alive at the time have passed down to posterity their particular genetic markers. Adam's line is the only one to have survived and proliferated.

A descendant of Adam identified by a mutation called "M94" was an inhabitant of the East African savannahs 75,000 years ago, and it was he who was the progenitor of most modern males because he was the founder of all haplogroups from B through R (haplogroup A did not leave Africa in ancient times). A later mutation on this male line called "M168" 60,000 years in the past is believed to have lived in an area that includes what is now Ethiopia in Africa, and he is the founder of haplogroups C through R.

To the north of Africa, according to Wells, an ice age was developing and drying up Africa's ecology to the extent that at least two groups that were descended from M168 migrated from Africa. The first group left around 60,000 years ago, and they are believed to have gone east following the southern coast of Asia populating southeast Asia, Australia, southern China, and the islands of the Pacific Ocean. A few appear to have been reunited with their by-then-distant kinsmen in North America about 10,000 years ago. A second wave of M168 emigrants from Africa traveled to the east and the north from the area of what is now the Sahara through Egypt and the Middle East.

A mutant marker on the M168 line called "M89" inhabited what became Mesopotamia and is now Iraq perhaps 45,000 years ago. As the founder of haplogroup F, this male was the ancestor of all the members of haplogroups G through R which include almost all Middle Eastern, European, Asian, and native American males. Several groups of M89 males traveled in various directions to a

---

[3]Wells, Spencer, *The Journey of Man — A Genetic Odyssey* (New York: Random House, 2004).

variety of places, but the founder of haplogroup G appears to have lived around 30,000 years ago in the area of the Indus Valley in what is now northern Pakistan and Afghanistan.

Up to around 10,000 years ago the members of haplogroups G through J were hunter-gatherers, but those people who lived in what is known as the "Fertile Crescent" developed agriculture, and "settled civilization" became possible — not only possible, but established, and disseminated far and wide. Populations expanded, farming and farmers followed the pioneers along the shores and through the islands of the Mediterranean, into the lands now called Turkey, the Balkans, and the Caucasus. The Indo-European language and its offshoots were soon to be found in northern India — including the Indus Valley — the Middle East, and Europe.

The Indus Valley civilization[4] was the largest of the four great early civilizations including Mesopotamia in the Fertile Crescent, Egypt, South Asia, and China, but it is the one that is least known and understood because, unlikely as it may seem, it was discovered only in the 1920s! How it was possible for modern mankind to live unwittingly among the ruins of this Indus civilization in one of the most populous regions of the Earth is confounding, but so they did, and still do. Archaeological researches are in their infancy there, and very little is known of the early tongues of the Indus because few language-bearing artifacts, most of them square stone seals with indecipherable symbols and animal motifs, have been found. So far, for lack of a Rosetta Stone, none of those scripts can be read, but we can recognize the animals, in particular the mythical unicorn, the bull, the rhinoceros, and the elephant. However, some of the major Indus cities have been identified and explored to a certain degree.

The first, Harappa, discovered in the western part of South Asia during the early nineteenth century, flourished from about 2600 to 1700 BCE. Its inhabitants built with bricks of the same size as were found in other Indus cities such as Mohenjo Daro and Dholavira. Harappa had well laid-out wide streets, public and private water supplies and distribution-drainage systems. Remnants of this Indus civilization exist in the south from the former Bombay in India to the Himalayas and Afghanistan in the north, and in the east from beyond New Delhi in Uttar Pradesh to Baluchistan, Pakistan, in the west, adjacent to the border of Iran.

---

[4]Indus River Valley civilization, etc., www.harappa.com/har/indus-saraswati.html.

Since there is evidence that trade existed between Mesopotamia and the Indus Valley Civilization, some of those members of haplogroup G living in its western portion must have gravitated toward the major centers of the Middle East. The westernmost Harappan site is Sutkagen Dor, located on the border of Pakistan and Iran on what once was, apparently, a navigable inlet of the Sea of Arabia and thus part of the trade route to Mesopotamia — in particular the fishing trade — between 3500 and 1700 BCE. This is the route, or one similar to it, that the early Turcos must have taken on their way to Sicily.

Gazing at a map of the world, one sees that a straight line drawn between the Indus River and a spot just below Sicily in what is now Tunisia, the ancient site of Carthage (not that our forebears followed anything like a straight line) crosses Iran (once Persia), Iraq (once Mesopotamia), Arabia, Jordan / Syria, Egypt, and Libya. Other modern countries in the area between the Indus and Tunisia are Turkmenistan, Azerbaijan, Armenia, Turkey, and Israel / Palestine.

Family Tree DNA is the name of the Internet organization that administers the DNA results of those people who have been tested and agreed to have their results publicly posted. Subgroups of FTDNA include organizations that follow individual haplogroups, including the Haplogroup G web group. There are other specialty groups including the Turk Name group, and the Sicily Project, to all three of which I belong. Peter Christy, administrator of the Haplogroup G organization, in an e-mail message dated October 27, 2006, wrote me, "Our haplogroup is seeking members from the Middle East and adjacent areas, but with little success. There are a number of 'high profile' members of the Saudi royal family, as well as a claimant to the throne of Iraq, Sharif Ali bin al-Hussein, that are members of Haplogroup G. Perhaps by your efforts to publicize our haplogroup in *Saudi Aramco World* [to the editors of which I wrote a letter on October 25, 2006, to which, as of February 8, 2007, I have not had a response], readers familiar with that part of the world may come to realize that they are a significant source of additional members.

"We have been attempting to contact those who have already been tested, but with little success. Bill Van Hemert has been using modal matching to profiles of known members of our haplogroup to find candidates who are registered at Ysearch. As you might expect, few of our emails even get through to the intended recipients and even fewer respond. All we have is some tantalizing clues left by a long list of potential Haplogroup G members with names that start 'Al-' e.g., Al-Blais, Al-Bukhary, Al-Khalili, Al-Kureishi, Al-Qureshi, Al-Rikabi, Al-Ruwaili, Al-

Sada, Al-Saman, Al-Shaibani, Al-Suwaidi and Al-Wazzan!"

The history of the swift spread of Islam is amazing. Muhammad was born in the Arabian city of Mecca circa 570 CE. Around 610 he experienced a revelatory vision, began to write what became the Koran, and in 613 he began to preach publicly. He left Mecca and settled in Medina in 622, and he died in 632 CE. Only sixty-five years later Islamic Arabs, many of them Moors — a mixture of Arabs and Berbers — lived in North Africa and occupied what was left of Carthage which had been destroyed in classical times and was again destroyed in 698. Today it is a wealthy suburb of Tunis.

In the ninth century CE, around 820, the Tunisian Arabs began to set up trading posts in Sicily. Incredibly, they were soon invited by Euphemius, a Byzantine general, to invade the island, and on June 13, 827, they did so from the town of Sousse, 120 km south of Carthage, with ten thousand infantry and seven hundred cavalry. According to Sandra Benjamin, "Although the invaders originated in many parts of the Muslim empire (including Spain), most of the men were Berbers (from the North African coast) and Arabs (from farther east)." Seventy-five years later, on August 1, 902, the Arabs captured Tauromenium, the Byzantine capital and the last unconquered Sicilian city. All the inhabitants were slain and the city burned to the ground.[5]

Surnames began to be used only about 1000 years ago, so the surname "Turco" dates from about 1000 CE, the eleventh century or 100 years after the Arab conquest of Sicily, that is to say about the same time as the Norman conquest of both England and Sicily. Sicily was the earlier to be conquered, by the brothers Hauteville, Robert the elder and Roger the younger who did most of the fighting, conquering Massena in 1061.

The Hautevilles' success is said to have inspired both the envy and ambition of their countryman William the Conqueror who invaded and subjugated England in 1066. Although he never ruled there, he pretended to the kingship of Sicily as well. It was William who ordered the Domesday Book of England to be written in 1086, and it was in this statistical survey that surnames were first assigned to every family. Something similar during this period was occurring throughout Europe, including Sicily.

---

[5]Benjamin, Sandra, *Sicily, Three Thousand Years of Human History* (Hanover: Steerforth P, 2006).

Michael Maddi who administers the FTDNA Sicily Project, in an e-mail message dated October 27, 2006, wrote me, "Have you noticed that out of 81 yDNA results in the Sicily Project, 10 are in the G haplogroup? That's about 12%. This has been the biggest surprise to me so far in our Sicily Project results. My guess, based on my previous reading, was that we would have maybe 5%.

"I have always wondered what the Arab contribution is to Sicily's genetic pool. It's hard to figure out how many people of Arab ancestry remained in Sicily after the crackdown by Frederick II on Muslims about 1230. (Frederick actually had good relations with Muslim rulers and spoke Arabic and appreciated the scientific knowledge promoted by Muslim scholars. It was the Vatican which demanded that he expel Muslims from Sicily.) One book I read recently [see Benjamin, *op. cit.*] said that 1/3 of Sicily's population was ethnically Arab when the Normans defeated the Muslim rulers around 1075. The town where my paternal grandparents were born, Mezzojuso, was founded by the Muslim rulers in the tenth century. It remained a majority Muslim town until about 1220, when Muslim rebellions in western Sicily and the subsequent crackdown led to many Muslims fleeing their towns for mountain refuges.

"I think our [haplogroup] G results, if they continue to stay above 10%, indicate that there is significant Arab deep ancestry in Sicilians and Sicilian-Americans."

The branch of the Turco family to which I belong has long resided in Riesi, a village in south-central Sicily. The closest city of any size is Licata, on the south coast. Although I know for a fact that a number of my relatives still live in the area, at the end of 2006 I was the only person worldwide with the surname Turco who has been identified through DNA analysis as belonging to haplogroup G2. (My son and my brother and his sons may be presumed to be members in this country.)

According to Halberts (*op. cit.*):

> Census records available disclose the fact that there are approximately 450 heads of households in the United States with the old and distinguished Turco name. The United States Census Bureau estimates that there are approximately 3.2 persons per household in America today which yields an approximate total of 1440 people in the United States carrying the Turco name. Although the figure seems relatively low, it does not signify the many important contributions that individuals bearing the Turco name have made to history.

In fact, although I am not so far as I know related to any of them, a survey of recent volumes of R. R. Bowker's *Books in Print* yields a seemingly disproportionate number of Turcos who are authors: Richard P. Turco is a science writer who has collaborated with Carl Sagan; Peggy Turco is a nature writer; Marco Turco writes travel books; Christopher Turco (not the Christopher who is my son, a musician) pens science fiction; Laura Lo Turco has written on the pyramids of Egypt; Ronald, on crime; Lorenzo Del Turco is an art historian; Vincent J. Turco publishes in the field of medicine; Douglas is a sports writer; Alfred is a scholar of English literature; Emanuele, diplomacy; Frank, food; Antonio, chemistry; Michael P., the Everglades; Page Turco is a media writer and performer; Salvatore J. is a nutritionist, and Mario Turco, a music historian. One recollects that the Moor on the Turco crest in his left hand wields a saber, but in his *right* he flourishes a scroll!

Apparently, none of these people has ever had his or her DNA tested. However, analysis shows that a person with a different surname, Frank Ricchiazzi of Laguna Beach, California, is rather closely related to my people although all of his family is from Montalbano, a suburb of Messina in the northeast corner of the island, and Santa Maria. (Is there a connection between this family name and the Arabic name Al-Rikabi mentioned above?) On December 11, 2006, he wrote in an e-mail message, "Clearly, our DNA shows a lineage going into the Indus region many centuries ago.

"Right now, I'm trying to find the time when my lineage first came to Montalbano. I have traced each grandparent to approximately 1500, but there does not appear to be any way to go beyond that date because I have exhausted the furthest points of the church records and the Rivelli in Palermo.

"My thought is that sometime in the late 1400's, there may be some information from the Kingdom of Two Sicilies that had a notation of a [member of my family] given some land in the Montalbano area. That of course means trying to locate some records from that Kingdom.

"One thing that you and I and others who do this research can say: Every day brings a new finding or another piece to the puzzles of who we are. Thank you for sharing your information."

The more people who have their DNA tested, the more pieces of the puzzle will be fitted into the mosaic of the deep ancestry of the family of humankind.

AN IMMIGRANT BALLAD

This poem was written while I was attending the University of Connecticut after I had graduated from Meriden High School in Connecticut and subsequently spent a four-year enlistment in the U. S. Navy. I talk about it a little in the memoir / short story "Father and Son," below, but others have written about it as well, in particular Jerre Mangione and Ben Morreale who reprinted it in *La Storia: Five Centuries of the Italian American Experience* (430–34; see my "Acknowledgments"),

My father came from Sicily
    (O sing a roundelay with me)
With cheeses in his pocket and
A crust of black bread in his hand.
He jumped ashore without a coat,
Without a friend or enemy,
Till Jesus nailed him by the throat.

My father came to Boston town
    (O tongue a catch and toss one down).
By day he plied a cobbler's awl,
By night he loitered on the mall.
He swigged his wine, he struck his note,
He wound the town up good and brown,
Till Jesus caught him by the throat.

He'd heard of Hell, he knew of sin
    (O pluck that wicked mandolin),
But they were for the gentle folk,
The cattle broken to the yoke.
He didn't need a Cross to tote:
His eyes were flame, his ears were tin,
Till Jesus nabbed him by the throat.

He met a Yankee girl one day
    (O cry a merry roundelay)
Who wouldn't do as she was bid,

But only what the good folk did.
She showed him how the church bells peal
Upon the narrow straitaway,
And Jesus nipped him by the heel.

My father heard a sermon said
    (O bite the bottle till it's dead).
He quit his job and went to school
And memorized the Golden Rule.
He drained his crock and sold his keg,
He swept the cobwebs from his head,
And Jesus hugged him by the leg.

The girl was pleased: she'd saved a soul
    (O light a stogie with a coal).
No longer need she be so wary:
Daddy went to seminary
To find how warm a Yankee grows
When she achieves her fondest goal.
And Jesus bit him on the nose.

At last he had a frock to wear
    (O hum a hymn and lip a prayer).
He hoisted Bible, sailed to search
For sheep to shear and for a church.
He asked the girl to share his life,
His choir-stall and shirt of hair,
For Jesus bade him take a wife.

My father holds a pulpit still
    (O I have had enough to swill).
His eye is tame, his hair is gray,
He can't recall a roundelay.
But he can preach, and he can quote
A verse or scripture, as you will,
Since Jesus took him by the throat.

Mangione and Morreale continued, "The humor here is strikingly reminiscent of Robert Canzoneri's novel *A Highly Ramified Tree* (1976). Canzoneri's father was also a Sicilian immigrant who married, in his case, not a Yankee but a southern woman, and he too became a minister in the Baptist Church.

"By 1990, after publishing his twelfth collection of poems, there is little or no evidence of the Italian experience in Turco other than the spelling of his surname. His recent collection of poetry, *The Shifting Web* (1990), is a far cry from the earlier poems about Italian Americans. One critic wrote of it: 'Dominated by images of snow, shadow, dust and decay, *Web* ignores urban life and human traffic. . . . Yet it is deeply philosophical.'"

Although I may not have written a great amount of poetry of late years specifically about "Italian Americans," I *have,* indeed, written a lot of prose about my Italian heritage, as this book and others attest.

THE STORY OF AN ITALIAN PROTESTANT

This is the story of my father told almost in his own words, with just a little elaboration and interpolation from me, but quite a fair amount of paraphrasing. It is a story that needs to be told because, as Charles J. Scalise wrote in his essay, "Retrieving 'WIPS': Exploring the Assimilation of White Italian Protestants in America," "This study explores the assimilation of the WIPS [an acronym taken by Prof. Scalise from his title phrase] into American culture and seeks to offer some possible explanations for their general invisibility in historical studies of Italian Americans."[1]

This is not the first time I have tampered with my father's work which I edited after his death in 1968 as *The Spiritual Autobiography of Luigi Turco* and donated in 1969 to the Center for Immigration Studies of the University of Minnesota at the request of its Director at that time, Rudolph J. Vecoli.[2] The manuscript consists of three parts, "A Brief Story of My Life," "The Wisdom of the Bible," and "A Letter to My Son" — that is to say, yours truly. After he had done his "Autobiography" and his "Letter," at the very end of his time, my father worked largely on translating some of my poems into Italian — not out of any literary consideration, but out of a desire to understand his older son. This is clear from some of his letters. He thought in Italian, and in order to communicate, he had first to translate his thoughts into English. The reverse was true as well — in order to understand English, he had to translate into Italian.

On several occasions, particularly in an earlier letter he had written me on September 16, 1957, he had asked me to help him out: "I am sending this copy to you of the story of my life for correction of my English. My greatest trouble is my English language. I am determined to master it as best as [*sic*] I can. So, please

---

[1]Scalise, Charles J., "Retrieving 'WIPS': Exploring the Assimilation of White Italian Protestants in America," *Italian Americana* 24.2 (Summer 2006) 133–46. [One does not understand why Prof. Scalise uses the "W" in his acronym, which is no more necessary than it is in "WASP" for "White Anglo-Saxon Protestant." How many varicolored Anglo-Saxons are there? "IP" would be enough, just as "ASP" is. And why does Scalese capitalize the "S"? It is a plural, not part of the acronym.]

[2]*Luigi Turco, The Spiritual Autobiography of,* ed. Lewis Turco. Available in photographic reproduction from University Microfilms International of Ann Arbor, Michigan, 1969.

teach me as much English as you can. Correct this paper for me and . . . show me all my mistakes of grammar, punctuation, construction, ect. [*sic*]."[3]

Luigi Turco was born in Riesi, a rural community in south central Sicily, on the 28th of May 1890. His surname means "Arab," and it dates from the period when, during the ninth and tenth centuries, Sicily was ruled by people who had derived from the Middle East (confirmed by a haplogroup G [M321] DNA analysis made by the National Geographic Society's Human Genome Project in 2006) and who entered Sicily from North Africa. No doubt that means his ancestors were Muslims.[4] However, "It goes without saying," he wrote, "that, being an Italian, my faith was that of the Roman Catholic Church."[5]

"It goes without saying." The assumption, even on the part of Prof. Scalise, is that all Italians, including Sicilians, are born members of the Roman church. The same assumption is without doubt made of all native Spanish, Portugese, French, and so on. Once, many years ago, my wife Jean — whose maiden surname was Houdlette, obviously French — met a young woman who was visiting from Brittany where she had had a parochial education. Somehow the subject of religion came up, and Jean said that her family had been Huguenots. The young woman had never heard the word, and when Jean told her that they were French Protestants, the woman was scandalized. "There are no Protestants in France!" she informed Jean, and no amount of assertion or argument could change her mind on the subject.

Just so in the case of Italians; however, my father continued, "Riesi is also the seat of a Waldensian Church. The Waldensians are the oldest Protestant group founded before the Reformation [before the word "Protestant" even existed], and the Waldensian Church in Italy may be considered as the National Protestant Church."[6]

The founder of the ancient sect known as Waldenses, a movement that opposed the ecclesiastical establishment, was Peter Waldo of Lyon (c. 1140–1217), a wealthy French merchant and religious reformer who began to preach during the twelfth century using as his text vernacular translations of the Gospels. His followers were known as the "poor men of Lyon," itinerant preachers who took a

---

[3] *Ibid.* xx–xxi.
[4] See the chapter titled "Muslims," 132ff, in Benjamin, op. cit.
[5] *Luigi Turco,* op. cit. 2.
[6] Benjamin, op. cit. 132.

vow of poverty and taught a simple, Bible-based type of religion, the sort that Prof. Scalise in his essay calls "evangelical."

In 1179 Waldo went to Rome to attend the third Lateran Council where his vow of poverty was confirmed by Pope Alexander III who, however, forbade him to preach. Nevertheless, he continued to do so, and subsequently, in 1184, he was excommunicated and banished from Lyon together with his followers. At the fourth Lateran Council of 1215 one of its seventy decrees condemned the Waldenses, and a second did the same to another group of sects, the Cathari, who followed the proscribed Manichaean doctrines.

Although by the late fourteenth century the Cathari had almost completely disappeared, the suppression of the Waldenses did not work, for they spread from France throughout Europe, including Italy, especially the Cottian Alps which now mark the border between Italy and France and are known still as the Waldensian Valleys. The Waldenses have over a hundred organized churches throughout Italy, one of these being that mentioned by Luigi Turco, located in Riesi, Sicily, seat of my father's family.

Thus, contrary to religious stereotyping, it is possible, if unlikely, for people in Italy to be born Protestant, just as they may be born Muslim or Jewish. And there is a third possibility. My father wrote, "My idea of Christianity, represented by both the Protestant and the Catholic people, was very vague. Until the age of twelve I never went to church; neither did any member of my family." This was unusual, because the stereotype for Sicily is that the men are indifferent to religion, as my father was, but at least the women attend church.[7]

Luigi Turco was conscripted for the Italian army when he was twenty years of age, and he served, ironically, for thirty months during the Turco-Italian war which was fought from 28 September 1911 to 18 October 1912. It was the first time he had left his village. He spent most of his enlistment in Rome, but even in the seat of the Catholic Church he was not enlightened, though he was troubled and beginning to seek enlightenment.

After his discharge he and his eldest sister, Vita Sardella, immigrated in April 1913 to the United States with her two boys, Joseph and Salvatore the younger. Her husband, Salvatore Sardella the elder, had preceded her by several years, and the family was reunited in Boston, Massachusetts. Unfortunately, Luigi's brother-in-law lived in a slum. Although in Sicily he had been a shoemaker, in America he

---

[7] *Luigi Turco,* op. cit. 2.

was anything but a success. He drank, he gambled, and he was laden with debts. Vita had to find a job just to put bread on the table, and so did Luigi, who paid his sister room and board.

Within a few months the family moved to a better neighborhood in Wakefield, not far from Boston. "By this time," Luigi wrote, "the hunger in me for a better moral and spiritual life was very deep. It had created in me a melancholic attitude, the spirit of despair! I tried to satisfy this hunger in me like the rest of the young people of my time, in drinking, eating, smoking, gambling, and other pleasures of the flesh, but to no avail. The activity of the Spirit upon me, then not clearly known to me, was leading me to find a better way, the real way, to satisfy the thirst of my soul for a better living."

Luigi discovered that in Wakefield there was an Italian Baptist church. One Sunday in July of 1915, when he was twenty-five years of age, he attended the morning worship service where the minister, Rev. Gaetano Lisi, preached a sermon in Italian. Something happened to Luigi during the course of that sermon. "My old way of living had died." When the service was over he spoke with Rev. Lisi, who sensed his earnestness, and shortly thereafter he found the force of will to stop smoking, drinking, and seeking illicit sexual experiences. Although the incident does not appear in his manuscript, he told me once that he also went on a liquid diet so as to purge his body of the poisons he had subjected it to.

"I became very enthusiastic in the work of the church," my father wrote. "The first desire of my heart was, of course, to lead my unreligious family in America and in Italy" along the path he himself had found. He began his missionary work at home with his sister and his two nephews, but Vita and her husband Salvatore balked, and they began a "terrific persecution" against Luigi because he had left the Catholic Church. However, when Vita noticed that her brother had actually changed his life's habits, as her husband had not, she began to be swayed. "Gradually she was converted, together with her family. They all became members of the Italian Baptist Church.

"Then," my father wrote, "I began to work for the conversion of my family in Italy. I wrote to my father . . . telling him and the rest of the family to go to the Waldensian Church, but he answered me negatively. He thought that I was [going mad]. I wrote to the minister of the church, Rev. Pietro Mingardi, an ex-monk of the Roman Catholic Church, to go and see my family and work for their conversion, but his efforts were not successful."

The First World War was in progress, but it wasn't until the last three months of the conflict that, for the second time in his young life, Luigi was drafted, this time into the American army. After the Armistice in November of 1918 he was discharged and returned to Wakefield and his sister's family. He found a job in a shoe factory in Lynn, Massachusetts, where he soon suffered an accident that cost him his right eye. Because his left eye was weak, he was nearly blind, and he was confronted with the dilemma of what to do for a living. The new minister of his church, the Rev. Theodore De Luca, suggested that Luigi study for the ministry himself. "I [had] wanted to work for God . . . but as a layman. Now I saw the light to . . . study for the ministry," not because *of* the accident, but because *in* the accident he saw that Providence had a plan for him.[8]

"At that time," my father wrote, "we had in Brooklyn, N[ew] Y[ork], the so-called Italian Department of Colgate Theological Seminary, of which Dr. Antonio Mangano was the head.[9] The course was five years long. The school took Italian immigrants who had been converted here from Catholicism to Protestantism. Practically all the students were men over twenty years of age with little education, so in the school the Italian and English languages were studied; an elementary American history, an elementary church history and theology; now and then some prominent man gave us a lecture on various subjects. I had gone to grammar school in Italy, and I was considered one of the best . . . students, so one may see that at the end of the course the men were not well prepared for the work of the ministry."

In the fall of 1919, after he had been attending the school for only a month, Luigi Turco was given the Italian Baptist Mission of Passaic, New Jersey. During the week he attended school, and he spent his weekends doing the work of the church in Passaic. Clearly, this was an early example, with a vengeance, of the system of internships that would later become popular in American higher education.

From the fall of 1924 to May of the following year Luigi and his seven fellow students spent the last year of the school with Dr. Mangano in Rome, Italy, studying at the Waldensian Seminary there. Luigi took advantage of the situation to visit his hometown, Riesi, several times.

His first visit took place during the second week of October. "Naturally," he wrote, "the minister of the church came to my home to see me and invite me to preach on the following Sunday. I accepted the invitation, of course! I had to

---

[8]*Ibid.* 3–4.
[9]Scalise, op. cit. 141.

preach for the evening service at 5 p. m. I went to the morning service together with my father and one of my brothers [certainly his older brother, also named Salvatore, not his younger brother Joseph]. There was a small group of people; about fourteen of them. I will never forget the words the minister uttered to me at the end of the service. He said, 'Brother Turco, you have no idea of the agony I am going through.' He was very discouraged. After years of hard work, the congregation of his church consisted of about 14 people.

"I preached in the evening service. Naturally, all the members of my family, and some of my relatives and friends, came to hear me. Even people of the neighborhood who knew me as a common young man going to America to make a fortune, and now back in Riesi, after twelve years, as a minister, came to see me preaching, just for the curiosity. The church was filled to its capacity. Over 150 people were present, which was a miracle for the minister and his small group. I preached as best I could, and I was delighted to see tears coming from the eyes of my father, [Salvatore] and mother [Rosaria Fasulo] and one of my brothers [Salvatore the younger]. It was a great joy for me to see such a crowd, but much more joy for the minister and the small group of people of his congregation, because in my coming they saw a revival in their church; they saw the rehabilitation of their missionary work."

Luigi Turco spent his Christmas vacation, the following Easter vacation, and the summer of 1925 as well, doing missionary work in Riesi. He went so far as to deliver a sermon at the jail where there was a young man he knew who was serving time. Luigi returned to the United States having converted his immediate family to Waldensianism as well as others of his relatives and a few friends. It amounted to a local revival of evangelical Protestantism and was the salvation of the Waldensian church in Riesi.

Returning to America, Luigi was assigned to be the pastor of the Second Italian Baptist Church of Buffalo, New York, but he continued to feel that his education was inadequate, and at the age of thirty-seven he entered high school while still attending to the duties of his ministry. He took his diploma in June of 1929; "then the idea came to me to go to college and to the regular seminary of Colgate-Rochester Divinity School. I finished my seminary work, but I did not finish my college work. I needed one more year to have my B. A. and my B. D. degrees," he wrote.[10]

---

[10]*Luigi Turco,* op. cit. 4–6.

While he was in Buffalo he talked his sister, Vita, into coming there to live with her family, minus the husband who continued in his unrepentant life style. Apparently Luigi managed this feat, which was huge in the family, while he was spending vacation time during the summers working among immigrant Italians in Wakefield. There he met and began to woo a not-so-young woman, May Putnam, ten years his junior, a Methodist missionary from Wisconsin and a member of an old New England family that had first come to unhappy prominence during the Salem witchcraft craze of 1692. She had overcome a family background of rural Midwestern poverty to return east to her family's origins to attend and graduate from the Boston University School of Religious Education. Elsewhere, I have written about her, and my father, as well.[11]

May and Luigi were married in 1933. I was born in 1934, and on February first of 1938, my father was appointed minister of the First Italian Baptist Church of Meriden, Connecticut, where I grew up and where my brother, Gene, was born in 1939. Luigi was pastor for seventeen years, until the age of sixty-two, the same year in which I graduated from Meriden High School in 1952 and thereupon enlisted in the Navy.[12]

This was not the end of my father's overall career, but I will leave it to those who are interested to pursue it in his manuscript *The Spiritual Autobiography* or in my books, *Shaking the Family Tree,* and *Fantaseers* (see note 11). I do, however, wish to return to Prof. Scalise's idea that WIPs are "invisible." My own career as a writer has not been invisible, yet it is true that the fact that I was born a Protestant is ignored for the most part, as is the possibility that there are French Protestants called Huguenots, or Italian Protestants called Waldensians. Discussing my poem "An Immigrant Ballad,"[13] about my father, Jerre Mangione and Ben Morreale wrote in *La Storia,* "The humor here is strikingly reminiscent of Robert Canzo - neri's novel *A Highly Ramified Tree* (1976). Canzoneri's father was also a Sicilian

[11]Turco, Lewis, "Mom May," 10–21; "Father and Son," 32–48, in *Shaking the Family Tree, A Remembrance* (West Lafayette: Bordighera, 1998); shorter versions, without poems, are included in *Fantaseers, A Book of Memories* (Scottsdale: Star Cloud P, 2005) 11–21; 31–45, respectively.

[12]*Luigi Turco,* op. cit. 7 8.

[13]Collected in my volume, *The Collected Lyrics of Lewis Turco / Wesli Court 1953- 2004* (Scottsdale: Star Cloud P, 2004) 8–9, together with a poem about my mother, "Requiem for a Name," 10–11, and one for my brother, Gene, "The Hustle," 173–74.

immigrant who married, in his case not a Yankee but a southern woman, and he too became a minister in the Baptist Church."[14]

A few pages earlier Mangione and Morreale had been discussing the late poet John Ciardi, whom I knew very well and counted a close friend.[15] Even he, who certainly knew better, forgot that I was the offspring of a mixed heritage marriage, because he wrote me in a letter dated February 28, 1979, in which he was fulminating against the idea of "Italian-American poets," not just American poets of whatever heritage, "I haven't heard from [Vince] Clemente. I have had a couple of over-breezy notes from Brian Swann [both of these poets have Italian backgrounds]. I really don't know what to make of so much Italo-Am. I've never thought in terms of I-Am poetry. I don't know any I-Am poets, as such. Lew Turco is an Am[erican] poet who happened to have It[alian]. parents."[16] No, like Swann, only one. And that's one reason why Italian-American Protestants are "invisible": because they may be only partly Italian, and the part that's not Italian can be anything. I remember that one of my former students, Markisan Naso, was half Italian and half Indonesian. If it's the father or the husband who is not Italian, the surname, too, can be anything.

I recall standing in front of the English Department mailboxes in Sheldon Hall at SUNY Oswego one day back in the 1970s when my colleague, Dorothy Park, came to stand beside me in order to retrieve her messages and memos. I happened to glance at a magazine she pulled out of her box and noticed that it was a copy of *The New Aurora* (*l'Aurora*), the official publication of the Italian Baptist Association of America, in which my father had published many articles and his Italian translation of my poem on the death of President John F. Kennedy.[17]

I was amazed. I asked if she were an Italian Baptist, and she replied in the affirmative. I would never have known if I'd not happened to be standing there at that moment. We began exchanging information, and we remembered all sorts of people and events that we had in common throughout our childhoods. We had even attended some of the same conventions with our parents. As an adult, she

---

[14]Mangione and Morreale, op. cit. 433.

[15]Turco, Lewis, "A Friend in Need, a Friend Indeed: A Memoir / Review," *Voices in Italian Americana* 9.1 (Spring 1998) 189–95; reprinted in *A Sheaf of Leaves: Literary Memoirs* (Scottsdale: Star Cloud P, 2004) 237–42.

[16]Cifelli, Edward M., ed., *The Selected Letters of John Ciardi* (Fayetteville: U of Arkansas P, 1991) 314.

[17]"November 22, 1963," *Poetry* 105.2 (Nov. 1964); Italian translation by Luigi Turco, "22 Novembre 1963," *The New Aurora* 63.3 (Nov. 1964).

had married into the prominent Park family of Buffalo, and her husband was a factory owner in western New York State. When she and I were growing up, the word among our generation was, "Assimilate!" And that's what we had done, though the idea of the Melting Pot is not a popular one nowadays.

Perhaps to take all these things into account requires too much ratiocination and critics find it easier to revert to stereotypes, as Dana Gioia did in an essay titled "What Is Italian-American Poetry?" where he assumes that all American poets of Italian ancestry have in their background the Roman Catholic experience.[18] Gioia — who is also a friend and, like Ciardi, certainly must know better in my case — is himself of mixed heritage: Italian and Portugese. No doubt he thinks that all Portugese-Americans, too, were born Roman Catholics.

Scalise quotes Mangione and Morreale (*q.v.*) to the effect that "For all of the Protestant efforts, fewer than 21,000 Italians converted."[19] It may be so, but how, at this date in the twenty-first century, would anybody be able to come up with an estimate of how many people of at least partial Italian background are currently converts to, or members of, another religion? My father's church eventually became the Grace Baptist Church because the members wanted to assimilate; later on, after one of those divisive squabbles that congregations are prone to, it split and the members of both sides began to attend other local churches. The Grace Baptist is no more.

In 1993, on one of my visits to Meriden, I went down to the corner of Windsor and Springdale Avenues to indulge nostalgia and take a look at my father's former church, both the original rectangular white clapboard wooden box sans steeple, and the newer, fancier structure built next to it after he retired (though he had raised most of the money for it during his pastorate).[20] Both were empty.

The old neighborhood is no longer predominately Italian but Hispanic. No doubt people believe that there is no such thing as a Spanish Protestant, either, but as I continued down Springdale I noticed across the street from the church and down a few storefronts, one of them had a sign in the window that read, "Spanish

---

[18]Gioia, Dana, "What Is Italian-American Poetry?" *Poetry Pilot,* newsletter of the Academy of American Poets (Nov.-Dec. 1991): 3–10.
[19]Scalise, op. cit. 134.
[20]Alfonsi, Ferdinando, ed. & tr., *Poeti Italo-Americani / Italo-American Poets,* a bi-lingual anthology (Catanzaro, Italy: Antonio Carello, 1985), "The Church," 394– 95. Also reprints and translates "November 22, 1963," 392–93 (see n17 above).

Baptist Mission." Perhaps in a few more years, if the congregation becomes prosperous enough, its members will purchase the property of both the First Italian Baptist Church and the later, Americanized, Grace Baptist Church on the corner. Perhaps they will name it "The First Spanish Baptist Church of Meriden, Connecticut." Like my father and his fellow apostates, they will be on their way to being invisible. Maybe "invisible" is good.

THE RECURRING DREAM

My father's story had come to haunt me by the time he was living in the house he and my mother had bought on South Avenue in Meriden after years of moving from one neighborhood to another, looking for an ever-cheaper rent in the last years of the Great Depression and during the Second World War. But the house in which I remember both of them best was the parsonage. We moved into it when I was in junior high school, before I went to Suffield Academy in Suffield, Connecticut, for the eighth and ninth grades. After years of planning and saving, the church had bought it, and for a while we had some feeling of physical location, a point of reference and a neighborhood.

One of the features of the house was the room I called the "sun-porch," though it was really merely an extension of the house that overlooked the driveway and the set of garages that the church rented out to neighbors who had no garages of their own. I had my aquaria set up there, and my father had his study behind some bookcases he used as a room divider. I would sit there for hours sometimes, musing into the aquaria, following the movements of my neon tetras, black mollies, and gouramis among the valisneria and swordplants. Sometimes my dad would be in his portion of the room reading, contemplating, writing his sermons. I would hear him moving quietly or tapping on his typewriter. For years after I had left the family for the Navy, marriage, college, I would dream of that room, the black angelfish swimming in the air. I have tried many times to write of it, in a story, and again in this poem:

  I seek my father — that minister
of the deep — among the furniture
    of my childhood. I step out of waking
  into this room and know
that time has passed. The windows are webbed
  and moonstreaked. A lamp with a glass shade,

  green and saffron, burns
on a brass stem. The bookcases hold sermons
    and silence. My aquaria
  stand among tumbled

tomes and testaments. The dust rises
into the amber darkness.

I disturb a desert of hours,
search for the fish that glide
in musty waters — blue scales
glint under my glance,
their eyes are corals budding
among rusty blades of sea grass

and swordplants. I remove the glass lids
and dip my hand into the water —
it is what I have feared:
shadow of a shadow, dim air
flowing from corner to corner.
The fish rise along the curtains

to swim about me in the air,
their black fins wavering.
I dig in the gravel stranded
among the shelving,
the decaying books. I dig,
and here, in the root

of the largest plant, blooming
from a socket of bone, I find my father
where he has scuttled,
at last to be brought back, smiling.

After I had finished this poem I thought that I had exorcised the dream, which was unsettling, though not a nightmare. I was wrong. The obsession continued, and continues to this day, forty years after father's death. My sleeping mind keeps trying to resurrect him, though he would be well over a hundred years old now.

A LETTER TO MY SON
by Luigi Turco

Meriden, Conn.
October 26, 1960

Dear Lewis,

Yes, dear, I am a dreamer, but I am happy to be one because I am realizing my dreams. Let me relate to you a few of my dreams which I have already realized. First the one concerning my two boys.

I presume that you know or have an Idea of my previous shattered romance before I married your mother. She was an Italian girl from a little church in Wakefield, Massachusetts, the small Italian Baptist Mission in which I was converted from Catholicism to Protestantism a few years after I came to the United States. She was the organist of the church and also a college student aiming for a superb career in the field of education. I sensed that she was interested in me and I responded, but never thinking to become serious because at the time I was a shoemaker with a simple elementary Italian education. In this situation, naturally, I did not dare propose to her; nevertheless, I enjoyed her friendship.

When she graduated from the State Teachers' College she found a teaching position in a Quincy grammar school. I think it was while she was in her first year of teaching that I lost my right eye in an accident in a Lynn shoe factory. It was my best eye — I had been wearing glasses because of the weakness of my left eye, so with the loss of the sight in my right eye I was almost a blind man.

The young lady, whom I shall call E., showed me tremendous sympathy. I was living at that time in the Wakefield home of my sister Vita Sardella. There I received almost every day numerous letters of sympathy from the children of the class E. was teaching. It touched my heart, but I did not dare to ask for her hand.

From the day of my conversion I had become deeply interested in the Christian religion. I wanted to master the point of view presented by Protestantism and the one given by Catholicism. I felt that Protestantism was superior because Catholicism had not helped me in Sicily. I had lived there until the age of twenty-three, and I never saw my parents or any member of my family go to church.

The only thing I heard about was the corruption of priests and nuns. I remember that nearby my home there was a priest who had four illegitimate children and I saw, with my own eyes, a priest during daytime going to see his woman. The profanity of language, especially in Riesi, was appalling to me. It was used in my own family by my father, not because he was a bad man, but because it is one of the bad habits of the Italian people. Like Dante I felt that I was not on the right lifetime path, and like him I perceived that if I continued to walk it I would come to disaster.

So, you can see, Lewis, why I became deeply interested in religion. I kept the Wakefield minister, Rev. Lisi, busy by asking him questions and for books to clarify my thinking about religion. I not only had to have a clear understanding about the Christian religion, but also to propagate it because it did so much good for my physical, moral, and spiritual life, and I wanted to help others who were as ignorant of it as I was. In my home, both in Wakefield and in Riesi, in factories, in streets, I was always looking for opportunities to speak about the Protestant Church, the only religion that presented the right point of view of Christianity for the salvation of the human race.

Seeing this zeal in me, Rev. Lisi constantly counseled me to study for the ministry, but I always refused to do so. I wanted to serve God as a good layman, and I wanted to do so especially because people were telling me that I was talking and preaching about religion because I wanted to become a minister. I wanted to prove to them that it was not so.

After my accident, while I was lying on a bed in the Lynn hospital, I prayed that God would give me the light and show me what to do next for my life's work. I knew that I was going to receive some insurance money, and I was thinking I might go back to Sicily and find there something to do to make a living and a way to dedicate part of my time to work for the Waldensian Church of Riesi. But it was not clear to me that that was what God wanted me to do. One day Rev. Lisi came to see me and kindly told me that it was time to quit resisting the call to study for the Christian ministry. I saw the light in his suggestion and I consented to do so.

At that time, 1920, there was a school called "The Italian Department of Colgate Theological Seminary" which was located in Brooklyn, New York, of which Dr. Antonio Mangano was the head. The aim of this seminary was to train young men of my type, immigrants converted from Catholicism, for the Italian Baptist Ministry.

You must understand that the normal education for a minister is three years in a regular seminary after he finishes his four years of college education. You can see, then, how poor an education I had. After the Italian grammar school education I received in Italy I jumped at the chance to study in an irregular seminary where they taught a little Italian, a little English, a little American history, and a little about theology and the Bible. The last year of the course, from October 1924 to May 1925 I spent in the Waldensian Seminary in Rome, Italy.

During that last year I had the opportunity to visit Riesi, first, two weeks before the school started, then during my Christmas and Easter vacations, and the entire summer of 1925. I had ample time to convert all my family to Protestantism and to create in Riesi a religious revival by preaching and teaching religion wherever I had the opportunity. I even went to the prison of Riesi to preach to the prisoners. I left Riesi during the month of August 1925, and I was assigned as pastor of the Trenton Avenue Italian Baptist Church, located in one of the worst slums of Buffalo, New York.

During this time I was not officially engaged to E., but there was a clear understanding that in the very near future we were going to be married. However, she had a brother in Wakefield who was quite a problem, not only to E., but also to her entire family, not a moral problem, but a social one. He was a shoemaker like me, but he wanted to be something better than a shoemaker, so E. asked me to call him to Buffalo and look for some kind of job for him.

I was occupying the entire four-room apartment of the church. This encouraged me to call him and let him sleep in my apartment without paying rent. At this time there was a huge group of recent Italian immigrants living in the neighborhood of the church. The Buffalo Board of Education was looking for an Italian who knew both Italian and English well enough to teach English to the newcomers. In order to begin a class it was necessary to have at least twelve people and a place where classes could be held. I said to the head of the Board of Education that I could easily fulfill those requirements, so he gave me the authority to go ahead with the plan.

When I knew for sure that I had twelve people, and of course the classroom space, I took the teacher, E.'s brother (whom I shall call S.) to meet the head of the Board of Education. S. was a handsome young man. He had not even finished high school, but he had a good mastery of the English language. He made a good impression upon the head of the Board of Education, especially when he discovered that S. was a shoemaker. Why? Because it was his intention to open a class in his system of schooling where boys could learn to repair shoes, so after a few weeks of teaching English to the immigrants in one of the rooms of my church S.

would also be regularly employed as a school teacher giving instruction in shoe repair. When I was in Buffalo last January for your cousin Salvatore Sardella's funeral, I heard that S. had just retired at about the age of sixty-eight.

S. had always been against my marrying his sister. One of the reasons for his opposition was that I had not a college education as E. did, and another was because I was a poor minister with a meager salary working in one of the worst slums of Buffalo. Since I had done him such tremendous good, I thought that I had placated his antagonism, but it was not so.

By this time even the American Baptist Missionary Society realized the mistake it had made in sending into the missionary field converted immigrants with such small preparation as mine; therefore, the Society raised its standards, and from that point it would require that only men with college and seminary educations could be employed in the Italian Baptist ministry. E. knew this, and one of the reasons for her hesitation in marrying me was just that, so very kindly she advised me to go to high school and then to college.

I accepted her suggestion! I wanted to be a hero. I wanted to marry her and show her and the rest of her family that they would not make a mistake by allowing E. to marry me. She had three more brothers who had a college education and one sister who was a school teacher too. Now another brother had become a teacher of shoe repair, so at the age of thirty-seven I went to high school in Buffalo, carrying the same work of my ministry, but with a reduced salary. I worked during the school year and summers among teen-aged boys and girls, and I finished my high school course in three years. Then I went to Rochester College and came back on weekends to do my church work.

Rochester is, I think, about seventy-five miles from Buffalo. There is located one of the most liberal seminaries, Colgate-Rochester Divinity School, so I thought I would do my seminary work first, take the three-year course, and then get married and finish my college work at the University of Buffalo. Thus, I could have achieved my two degrees, the B. A. and the B. D.

I finished my seminary work, and I finished one year of college work as well. I was forty-three by then, and felt it was time for us to be married after ten years of an unofficial engagement. But E. was always hesitating and I knew that it was not only because of my lack of a college education, but also because I was a minister. She had a great admiration for me, for my character, but not for my profession, because her father had died a religious fanatic. She had an idea that I was also a fanatic.

Lewis, dear, I never wanted to be a religious fanatic, but I wanted to be an intelligent religious minister. I never was satisfied with the idea that life consisted in living three-score years and ten and then end in oblivion. I never was satisfied to believe that life consisted in a terrific struggle to make a living. I wanted to know what was my connection or relationship with what science calls "the principle of life," or "first cause"; what philosophy calls "the reality of life," or what religion calls "God."

My understanding of life, then, is beautifully expressed in your poem, "A Hollow Rush":

it goes away, leola,
    as the rabble hooves have gone:
        the prairies linger.
none, no, none may know
    the sable mane for long,
        nor the stallion's great desire.
the souls of brontosaurs may run
    their feather course
        for all I know, leola.
this is true, though:
    oceans dwell
        among the continents.
look through a hollow rush,
    leola; sight is limited
        and vaguely dry.
peer through your flesh
    or mine, leola —
        what do you see?

It was exactly the way I was looking at life then, as "A Hollow Rush," a worthless existence and an unintelligent and rash preparation for it, but E. would not see it. She had a one-track mind — the father died a religious fanatic, and she was afraid that the same thing was going to take place with her husband, but I pressed the idea of marriage — or else! Finally she came to a decision, but on one condition. What was it?

She wrote to me that her family physician had told her that her genital organs were weak, therefore she could not bear children. She told me, too, that I could enjoy sexual intercourse with her just the same, and if we wanted children we could adopt some. That was very disgusting to me. I knew that the primary function of sexual relations is for procreation and not only for the simple reason of pleasure; besides, I wanted children of my own. I told her that the end of our romance had arrived.

A year before the final break I had met your mother in a children's camp near Boston, conducted by the Italian Methodist Church of that city, of which Salvatore Giambarresi, A Riesino, was the minister. Your future mother was a missionary there. I had fallen in love with her, but I did not dare to propose to her because I still had a good relationship with E., but when I broke the engagement I lost no time before writing to Miss May Putnam expressing my interest in her. She accepted my proposal on one condition. What was the condition? That she wanted to be a mother! This naturally delighted me because I myself wanted to be a father. Within five months we were married. I was forty-three at that time, and your mother was thirty-four. A year later you were born; then, after five more years, your brother Gene was born.

It has been my prayer to live long enough and have enough income to see my two boys well educated and well settled in life. My dream has been realized with you, my first son, and with Gene, partially realized. I will never forget it when you said, during one of our domestic conflicts, "Daddy, I will never bring disgrace home." No, you have not. You have brought honor to your family, to your wife's family, to every place where you have gone, and now you will bring honor to the school where you are teaching and to the city of Cleveland. I was very pleased to read in your last letter that you are very happy there and well established.

Gene, more or less, has expressed similar sentiments that, knowing he comes from a good family, he will never allow himself to do something which will disgrace himself and us. I will never forget a letter which he received from a lady of a nearby town. It was late at night. Nobody was around when Gene damaged a car parked in front of that lady's house. Gene could have gone away without being caught, but no, that was not the right action. Following his inner light he went and knocked at the door of the house where the lady lived and told her he was ready to pay the damage amounting to about fourteen or twenty dollars — I do not remember the exact amount. The woman was astounded by his honesty. A couple of days afterwards she sent the bill along with a letter filled with admiration telling him that he had set a marvelous example for her children and praising us, Gene's parents, for having such an outstanding boy.

Yes, God has given the joy of seeing you well settled, now He will give me the joy of seeing Gene well settled, too. He is well settled. He has a wonderful, respectable job as a toolmaker, and he is taking college courses to become a mechanical engineer, but I want to see him married with children, like you.

Now let me relate to you another dream which I have realized, the dream for the intellectual education of my entire family here in America and in Riesi.

When I was in Riesi in 1924–25, besides leading my family to accept Protestantism as their religion, it was also my dream to elevate all the members of my family in their intellectual life. To this aim I bought two bookcases, and one for my sister Beatrice's family, Fina's mother, who had six children. I furnished the two bookcases with a few books. During my stay in Riesi then there was a school teacher, and I told my brother Joseph to court that young lady. He laughed at me because he was an uneducated shoemaker, and it would be presumptuous of him to follow my advice. But I told him to go ahead because with a brother who was a minister now his prestige in life had increased. I left Riesi and was very pleased a year later to hear that Joseph had won the young lady. They had two children, a boy and a girl. The girl is a school teacher, and the boy graduated this year as a surveyor.

Now let me speak to you of my sister Beatrice's six children. Her husband, too, was a shoemaker, and a very poor one. In a rural town such as Riesi, the boys learn the trade of their father, and the girls help the mother in her housework. Those who can afford it, and you find a very few of them, send their children out of town for a higher education. My sister Beatrice found a way to get her two boys out of the shoemaker shop of her husband and inspire them to study. The means? Well, she managed to find some way, and now one of the two boys, Salvatore, is a school teacher.

The other, Felice, became a priest, a professor of theology in the Catholic seminary in Caltanissetta. Like all the priests there, he is deeply interested in the Christian Democratic Party of Italy, and I understand that he is one of the most quoted politicians in the country. Before I left for my return visit to Riesi in 1954 I was pleased to hear from him that he owed to me his inspiration to be a priest, for while I was in Riesi in 1925 I created a great revival not only for the Waldensian church, but also for the Roman Catholic, and my nephew Felice was one of its products. His sister Sarina, who remained strong in the Protestant church in spite of the pleas of her brother to leave it and to embrace Catholicism again, told me last year that I had been of inspiration, comfort and courage to her in pursuing her study in her maturity. She, too, is a school teacher.

I could say the same thing of the children of my older sister Vita. Her husband, too, was a shoemaker, but the worst part of him was his character. He was a drunkard and a gambler. His aim was to exploit his children. But, again, under my guidance Vita's children are what you know they are. When I was in Buffalo one night I had a telephone call from my nephew, Vita's son Salvatore, who was at the Buffalo railway station. When I went to pick him up he told me that his father had almost killed him by throwing a pressing iron at him. He could not get along with his father, so he stayed with me. He found a job, and he began to work; afterwards, he became inspired by seeing me at work among the poor Italian people of Trenton Avenue, helping them in any way possible through the Salvation Army, Welfare Service, Goodwill Industries, etc., to study to be a minister. I sent him to school, but he changed his mind and decided to become a school teacher.

So, you see, Lewis dear, that some of my dreams have been realized. The next dream that I wish to realize is the removal altogether of the void or the "Hollow Rush" of my soul. The metaphysical understanding of the Bible is helping me to do it.

Yes, dear, I would like to come to Cleveland and spend some time with you and with your dear family, but not until I close for the summer the church that I began in the ballroom of the old hotel downtown here in Meriden when I was forced to retire. It is true I have not many people attending, but now I am helping a lady here in Meriden to remove her fear of life. Another woman and her daughter, with another young man, come from New Haven to hear my sermons, and they tell me that they receive some benefit from them.

Sometimes I am alone in the church with your brother Gene, but I am very happy to chat and preach a sermon for him. This church is helping me tremendously in my spiritual realization, in my evolution to become like Jesus, the Son God sent to Earth to help in the establishment of His kingdom, the kingdom of "peace on Earth and good will toward men."

May God bless you, dear, together with your family. Many kisses to my granddaughter Melora. With

Love your father,
Luigi

THE CHURCH

Needless to say, "the church" loomed exceedingly large in my life. If we as a family were poor, and we were, so was the parish. As a result, I had not only to attend Sunday school, Vacation Bible School, the weekly sermon — at least the one in English, for my father preached two services, one in Italian as well — and sing in the choir when I was old enough, I also had to mow the big lawn in the summertime and shovel the walks in winter. Eventually, when papa could no longer find a volunteer parishioner to do the job, I became the official janitor for the church, and that meant that I got paid a pittance for doing everything a janitor does. If my father had realized what one of my tasks led to, he would have fallen to his knees and begged the Lord to forgive him.

In the basement it is cool
among the tables, the small chairs,
the folding screens and crayons.
The lavatory is damp, the water runs;
there is room for webs and fables.

The wooden stair ascends and turns
into heat settled among the pews.
The altar rises above the golden oak
which dark juice has stained.
Frayed wine runs down the center aisle
away from the electric keys,
the hymnals with the broken covers.

Summer lies upon the step before the door,
beneath the white clapboards,
the pictures peeling from the glass.
The gate of pipe and wire stands ajar.

Next door the parsonage is scaled to dolls.
It takes the corner,
facing another neighborhood.
Six garages stand by a gravel drive.
A pear tree withers there, and on the curb

an elm like a cathedral stays alive.

Being both a Baptist and an Italian posed certain insoluble dilemmas for my father, but not for my Methodist mother. Both denominations eschewed alcohol, including wine, but wine is a staple for Italians. At home there was never a problem, because neither of my parents drank at all. However, if there were a wedding at which my father officiated, at the reception following he was expected to lead a toast to the bride and groom, and everyone was supposed to make the toast with real wine.

I remember once when my mother publicly belabored my father at a reception for drinking a sip of the toasting liquid. My mother had no tact at all. With the parishioners and guests looking on, a public dust-up took place between May and Luigi of the sort that they, my brother Gene, and I were very well used to, but my father was humiliated, and that's not too strong a word. He was enraged. The wedding party was appalled, primarily with mother.

Early on Communion Sunday mornings I would go out the back door of the parsonage, walk a few steps, go into the side door of the church, down a few steps, and into the basement where the kitchen was located. I had to cut up a loaf of Wonder Bread into cubes, put them on trays, and fill the little communion wine glasses not with wine, but with grape juice; then I had to carry the trays of bread and juice upstairs and place them on the communion table for the ushers to distribute. The parishioners would take bread and "wine" from the trays the ushers passed around, and then place the used glasses into the cup holders on the backs of the pews.

Afterward I had to collect the cups again, place them into the trays, and when I got back to the kitchen I had to separate those that had been unused and remained untouched in the trays. Then, using a funnel, I poured the untouched grape juice back into the bottles which, as I recall, were not refrigerated, though I may be wrong about that. I was not above sampling some of the little glasses instead of frugally saving their contents for the next month's communion.

One day while I was sipping a few my head began to feel odd, sort of dizzy and muzzy. I picked up one of the bottles and held it up to the light. I noticed that there was something in the bottom of the bottle, something fuzzy, sort of, a bit like furry marbles. I sniffed the open neck — it still smelled like grape juice, but there was another element besides grape, a sort of robust body with an autumn finish and overtones of spice.

I staggered back to the parsonage and probably went to the room I shared with my brother. I don't believe I alerted my father to the situation with the weird grape juice because, as I recollect, I did the same thing more than once. On the other hand, I don't remember that this particular chore of mine lasted very long. If I had to give odds, I'd bet that my ever-vigilant mother finally caught on. Once, when I was a man, she got after me for carrying Bay Rum around with me in my travel kit. I had the Devil of a time convincing her that Bay Rum is an after-shave lotion.

LEMON ICE

Pick a day, just any summer day between 1945 and 1947. The sun is boiling down through the big elm on the corner of Springdale and Windsor Avenues in Meriden, Connecticut, and Lewis is sitting on the front steps of the parsonage looking across Windsor at the run-down corner grocery store, Galluzzo's Market. If he shifts his gaze and looks right, to the northern corner, he will see another grocery — not quite so run-down, not quite so large — Cotrona's.

In the house behind Lewis his father, Luigi, is hard at work on his English and Italian language sermons for the coming Sunday. Lewis's father will deliver his sermons from the pulpit of the white clapboard First Italian Baptist Church behind the house, facing Springdale, surrounded by a wire fence. It is a box of wood without even a steeple, but the churchyard is a large one — Lewis should know, he has to mow the lawn once a week. On it the church each summer holds its Strawberry Festival, the chief attraction of which is not the strawberry shortcake but the Italian pastries sold at the booths manned by large Italian women and patronized by slender Italian men and loud Italian-American children.

The church and parsonage literally and figuratively straddle the corner where Italian and German neighborhoods collide in a melee of great trees and No Parking signs. The whispers of the Roman Catholic neighborhood of Springdale have it that these renegade Protestant Eyetalians are holy rollers. The funny little Sicilian priest had wanted to marry some Mayflower queen. They drink real blood, not grapejuice, in those shot glasses. They hire a band to praise the Lord — but the band isn't hired, for Elsie plays the new Hammond and old Mr. Parisi brings his fiddle to church on special days. Somebody puffs into his trumpet, somebody else has an accordion, and the noise is always lovely.

In the days of their early childhood Lewis and his brother Gene used to swing on the church gate made of wire and silver tubing. There always seemed to be a bully around to spoil their fun and to challenge them as they rode the barrier that sealed the churchyard off from the neighborhood. "Let's see you spit on the stairs," he might dare Lewis. "You're scared, punk. Your old man eats snails. Where do you people keep the snakes you kiss on Sunday?"

Lewis's mother is somewhere indoors working on the laundry or the floors, perhaps. She is the unhappy one. A midwest farm girl who worked her way out of the fields her father let go to seed, who struggled her way through college to become a missionary among the immigrant Italians, she had married one of them and lost the status she had fought and scrambled for.

Lewis's younger brother, Gene, is lurking around somewhere, no doubt planning to horn in on whatever Lewis eventually does. What he is planning is getting over to the lemon ice store. The problem is lack of money, but Lewis believes he has solved it.

He gets up and walks slowly across the patch of green lawn under the elm, around the end of the fence at the corner, and cuts across Springdale. Inside Cotrona's it is cool and the smell is of sawdust and salami — the sawdust is sprinkled across the floor, and the salamis hang with the cheeses from wires stretched across the ceiling. There are kegs of olives in the aisle. Behind the counter stands Frank Cotrona minding the store for his father. As usual, the store is otherwise empty of customers.

"Did y' come over to go a couple rounds?" Frankie asks, grinning. Lewis nods. Frank and he are the same age, but Frank is bigger. "Same deal? Three rounds for a nickel bag of chips?" Lewis shakes his head. Frankie's smile disappears. "What, then?" He leans his elbows over the counter and looks at Lewis, his pompadour flopping over his dark eyes.

"Three rounds for a nickel," Lewis says.

"A nickel!" Frank wails and straightens up. "The priest's kid has gone pro!" His eyes are fake wide. Frankie and Lewis stand there staring at each other for a minute. "Okay," Frankie says, "it's a deal."

Frank comes around the counter untying his white apron. They square off, hands open. Frank zips one in and taps Lewis on the cheek. He laughs. "Come on, Turk, earn your money." Frank has a longer reach.

Lewis gets mad at all the little taps and goes windmilling in.

Frankie backs off laughing and defending himself. "Okay, okay, that's your round," he says. He hauls a dime out of his pocket and hands it to his sparring partner. "Six rounds, and I throw in a nickel bag of chips," he says. The match resumes.

"Thanks, Frank," Lewis says pocketing the cash at last. They shake. Frankie goes back behind the counter as Lewis goes out and closes the door behind him.

He turns left. There's a house next door on Springdale, then Ponzillo's Tavern, the bone in his father's craw, for it is almost across the street from the church. This is a place that ranks in fable in the Italian community of Springdale, but not in the mythology of the Germans and mixed breeds of Windsor. This is the house and store-front where the Gallicized Ponselle sisters were raised, the only divas Meriden ever produced. Lewis knows this, but he doesn't know why their name is Ponselle, not Ponzillo, and he has never heard them sing, for Rosa Ponselle's years of glory had been over for nearly a decade and a half. She had stopped singing at the Metropolitan in 1937, when Lewis was three years old and still living in Buffalo. Luigi loves opera, but Lewis won't listen to it when it is played on the radio or the wind-up phonograph.

Next door is the lemon ice store. "Agostino's Fish" it says on the dusty window, but Lewis has never seen a fish inside. His throat is as dry as the last leaf, and the sun is hotter than ever. He goes in, the bell on a jiggler over the door makes its Christmas sound — "Allo, boy," Mrs. Agostino says, smiling, the faint mustache over her lip arching like the back of a cat. She sits in a chair beside the ice-cream freezer, in front of the window. The candy counter is against the back wall, and behind it is the lemon ice machine: a wooden bucket containing a smaller metal vat that has a top with a gear. Over this fits another gear on a drive-wheel, the whole thing hooked to an electric motor. Ice, sugar, and lemons go inside, ice and salt go outside, the motor goes round. It is not going round now. Mr. Agostino — large, not terribly friendly — is putting together the ingredients.

It has been many years since this childless couple stepped off the boat to find the fortune to be found in an antique motor and tub, in ice, sugar, and lemons, in paper accordion cups one can squeeze the flavor out of. If you eat too fast the most excruciating headache will momentarily blind you as pain spreads through and across your sinuses. When you are done with the ache and the lemon ice you throw the cup away on the summer sidewalk outside where the kids have collected maybe to play ball or break a window or go walking down the street full of slat-frame one- or two-decker houses, some with a cat on a strip of earth looking out for the family dog through the spokes of a rusty trike between the weedy steps and the feet of passers-by, the phone poles growing their vines through the leafless breeze scuttling newsprint along the street, the grainy shingles knocked up underneath some old living room turned into a grocery store where all the cornflake boxes on the shelves host banqueting black specks that scatter in the bowl after the rustling has stopped.

"You got a lemon ice?" Lewis asks.

He is out of luck. Mrs. Agostino shakes her head. "We makin' somma now," she says, "'bout a half-hou'. You come back, eh?" Lewis stands still, deeply hurt, deeply frustrated. How can fate be so unrelenting? Mrs. Agostino understands. "You wanna Milky Way?" she asks. Lewis shakes his head and shows her his single dime. "Wella, half-hou'," she says again. "That'sa no so long."

The shadows in the shop gather heat to themselves and smother the corners of the store. In the counter only the hard candies are not in immediate danger of melting — the dots of candy on long strips of paper, the sour balls. All the rest — the jelly hats, the Baby Ruths — may not survive a half hour, no more than Lewis will. He turns to leave just as the bell rings again.

"Oh, no! What do you want?" Lewis asks. It is Gene standing in the doorway.

"Lemon ice," he says.

"They're out. Let's go." He starts to push by his brother, then stops. "Where'd you get the money?" Gene drops his eyes. "You don't have any, right?"

"Where'd you get yours?" Gene asks.

"Hey, you kids!" Mr. Agostino yells, "Closa da door. Da flies comin' in!"

Lewis grabs Gene by the arm and yanks him outside. "You never mind where I got mine," he says. "That's a secret."

"You been boxing with Frankie?"

Lewis can feel the gorge rising in his throat. It's bad enough that he's dry and hurt, now he's mad. He shoves Gene again, hard this time, hard enough to knock him down. Gene scrapes his knee and starts to cry. Lewis crosses the street, opens the church gate and latches it behind him — Gene doesn't know how to get the two halves to go back together right and get the vertical bolt to fit into the round hole in the pavement. Lewis glances back and sees Gene picking himself up and heading for the corner to cross toward the front yard. By the time he gets there Lewis will be long gone.

Lewis opens the gate again, crosses the street, and starts walking down the block along Springdale, past houses and shops, until he reaches Bonanzinga's Bakery where, if it were autumn, he could loaf on a cool day and watch the bread brown in the stone oven stoked with coal.

The loaves leave the oven on a long wooden spatula as Enrico's arms, like brown loaves themselves, move in and out among the rustlings of the narrow white bags. There is a measured bustle in the bakery. "Eh!" Enrico might say, "make some dough; make some more dough." And so they make some dough — they mix it, they knead it, they cut it, they mold it, then into the oven to bake it. Lewis buys it, hot, for a quarter — hot, for they would be waiting at home. "Go!"

says Enrico, "go, run! Bread gets cold quick on a cool day."

This, though, is anything but a cool day. On days when it is very hot in the sunny streets like this and the gang languishes after lunch and the morning games, Lewis and his friends might continue down the block to Lewis Avenue, sluggish with heat, and turn left. There, parked at the curb, across the street and two storefronts down from where Lewis had lived when he was in kindergarten, would be the ice-house on wheels.

When they come to the dreamy door that roars its crystal silence into the sun; where the cubes of sawdust winter rest waiting for the fellows to pick up chips to suck; when they come to that best of quiet doors, there Guido sits with his hat pulled down, and his eyelids pulled down as well, and the shadows down, down to his knees like an awning's ghost. There is no movement, not even of his lips, as Guido says, "Welcome, boys. Come in, get cool. Get cool near the ice, boys," Guido says.

Across Lewis Avenue, on the opposite corner of Springdale, there is the establishment of Louie the barber. When Lewis was five all he had to do was cross the street cater-corner to get to the barbershop. There, Louie would lower the boom on the boys' cowlicks and locks. As Lewis walked in he'd get a snootful of pomade smells — Vitalis, Wild Root Cream Oil, Charley. He'd sit in the leather-upholstered, white porcelain, pneumatic chair, his head bent forward on his chest while Louie snipped and combed. Lewis would be thinking, perhaps, of the bats thwacking in the back lot while he sat there itching and the mirror near the chair beckoned him to move . . . just once.

"Well, the Yanks won," Louie would say, "yes, the Yanks won and the Sox lost. What grade you in now, sonny? Steady now, steady your head . . . one more swipe with the comb . . . wish I could comb my hair," said Louie. "See?" He'd lower his bald pate to be patted. "Bene, bene, go home now. You're done, you're ready for church tomorrow. Next man, who's next? Who's next?" asked Louie.

Lewis crosses Springdale and turns back toward home. If he stops at Tomassetti's Market about a third of the way down the block he will find Mr. Tomassetti, the father of Mario and Eddie, two kids from the church who were about Lewis's own age, spraying lambchops out from under his snickersnee as though he were some gory potentate mucking his way to empire through the limbs of his enemies.

Underfoot the going is unsteady, for the floor is covered with wood shavings that slide up to the showcases that hold a museum of meat that reminds Lewis of his collections at home. Mr. Tomassetti rises in all his charnel glory from behind the chopping block, lays down a bouquet of ribs, perhaps. The bow of his apron ties off his rump where a man's back should start above the buttocks.

"How many you want?" the butcher says to a housewife, "how many pork chops you want? These will go nice in a big pot of sauce. That's prime pork, Mrs. Spinelli.

"Here, boy, have some chips and run along, I got work," he might say to Lewis when his customer, another parishioner, has left. "Give my respects to your father." He would move, maybe, toward the coldroom door, open it, and disappear into its intoxicating coolness.

At last it is time. Lewis drags his feet through the suffocating heat back toward Agostino's candy store. While he has been walking Lewis has been thinking about many things: What will it be like when he has gotten to high school finally? What will he turn into at last, a moth or a butterfly? But mostly about the lemon ice. His lips have puckered and his mouth has tried to water, but his throat is a column of aching parchment.

While he has been waiting, has it gotten cooler? It is almost as though he is inhabiting two different days at the same time, for yes — he has felt the breath of autumn stirring and rustling among the leaves. He has felt the roughness of gooseflesh upon his arms, and he has shivered. Now, crossing the avenue, jaywalking past the church, he looks down at the pavement and feels as though his eyes are farther from it, as though there is a further distance between him and the earth. It is as though there were a piece of glass between his vision and the envisioned, a sheet of glass not quite clear, slightly tinted, so subtly colored that he could almost, but not quite, swear there is nothing there at all. He stops to kneel, to bend and tie his shoe — it does not truly need tying, but he wants to see if the distance he is experiencing is physical.

It is not. Nothing changes, although he can feel the movement of change all about him. He shakes his head as though to clear it, rises, and walks on. He comes to the door of the shop and goes in, and then he feels it strongly.

He looks at Mrs. Agostino and notices for the first time what she is wearing — it is a long black dress made of some sort of semi-shiny material, not the usual house dress and apron. On her head there is a close-fitting hat with a black veil falling from it. There is lace trimming here and there about her person — it reminds Lewis of webs.

He looks at Mrs. Agostino, but he cannot tell whether she is returning his gaze. “One lemon ice, please,” he says, holding out his money.

The old woman shakes her head. “We no got,” she says, “no got no more. You want some candy, maybe?” She begins to go to the counter, but Lewis shakes his head, an enormous sorrow settling into the pit of his stomach to reside with the hunger and thirst already there. Lewis glances back at the window whose thin film of dust is a deeper tint of the glass he had imagined while he was crossing the street. Now he knows why Mrs. Agostino’s veils and laces remind him of webs, for there are webs in the corners of the store, and the floor is littered with scraps of paper, even an empty pop bottle or two.

Lewis looks at the chair behind the counter where Mr. Agostino always sat tending or guarding the machine, but the seat is empty.

The flat cushion is faded and threadbare. The machine itself is empty, the gears rusty, the wood dry and stained. Lewis knows, but does not understand how he knows, that Mr. Agostino is gone for good. How can that be? He had been in the store barely a half-hour earlier.

Mrs. Agostino shuffles back to her own stool by the window, sits down, and turns her head as though to look into the street. She says nothing more. Lewis sees her hand in her lap lying palm up, the tips of the fingers trembling slightly, every now and again the whole hand giving a fitful jerk. The old lady is more stooped than ever, Lewis thinks. He stands until he begins to feel embarrassed, and then he turns to the door, opens it — the bell makes no sound beyond a small clunk as the door hits it. Lewis looks at it to see what is the matter. It has no tongue.

Outdoors it is autumn. The church and parsonage look the same, but Lewis can feel the difference — no one he knows is inside. The aquaria with his tropical fish in them no longer line the shelves before the windows of the sunporch. The guppies and betas have risen through the glass lids and swum away into thin air. His father writes his sermons no longer in the study where the green-shaded brass lamp stood on his desk throwing a yellow light upon the words about God, words that have long since browned into umber. Who knows where his mother has gone, where his brother is now?

It is autumn. Behind him the candy store stands with its door locked, the window papered over. Cotrona’s market is closed, too, and so is Galuzzo’s which had used to be . . . hadn’t it turned into? . . . a pizza palace. Lewis’s mouth is as dry as the last leaf in a book of leaves. Who knows where he is now? Perhaps it is no longer even autumn.

REQUIEM FOR A NAME

For as long as I have known the meaning and origin of my surname, I have known about the Putnams of Salem, Massachusetts, and their involvement in the Witch Hunt of 1692. Luigi Turco met May Laura Putnam — "Mom May" as she liked to call herself, because of the pun, I suppose — at a Methodist camp in Wakefield, Massachusetts, where she was working as a missionary among Italian immigrants. At the time she was an old maid in her thirties who had pulled herself out of rural poverty in Superior, Wisconsin, by sheer wit and strength of will. Despite the desperate penury of her second generation Danish mother, born Laura Christine Larsen; the shiftlessness of her father, William Herbert Putnam, descendant of an old New England family, and the competition of her six brothers and two sisters, Mom May had made something of herself, becoming the only one of the Putnam siblings to attend and graduate from college — Boston University's School of Religious Education.

Believe it or believe it not,
        My mother was a Putnam once.
    On her ancestral tree she swears
The Lowells and the Deweys too
    Hang pendulous as lovely pears.
        My grampaw was a sort of dunce
Who rather let things go to pot —

Himself, his offspring, farm and wife.
        My grampaw was a sort of dunce.
    His homestead I remember well:
The floors were warped, the doors askew,
    And now and then the rafters fell.
        My mother was a Putnam once —
She led a less than social life,

So she went East from grampaw's West.
        My mother was a Putnam once
    Till she was married, woe O! woe.
No longer was she maiden free —

She cursed her pa from pate to toe.
My grampaw was a sort of dunce
To cheat the eaglet in its nest

By willing her a woman's form.
My grampaw was a sort of dunce,
But what a hefty name he wore!
He gave my middle name to me;
It fits me like a saddlesore.
My mother was a Putnam once,
I'd be one too, come sun or storm.

The Deweys and the Lowell hosts
Are pendant from a hollow tree.
Now with this rime let them be felled,
Let them be nothing more to me
Than windfalls blasted by the frosts.

My mother was a Putnam once;
My grampaw was a sort of dunce.

Mom May was wrong about the Lowells, but right about the Deweys.

So my parents married and I was born into their middle age. We lived a while in Buffalo near my father's sister, Vita Sardella, and her family. I was christened Lewis (my mother was having no other "Luigi" in the family) Putnam (hyphenated last names were not yet current in the U.S.) Turco, and then we moved to Meriden, where I was brought up unaware of how poor we were. Thinking back on my early life, I consider it remarkable that my parents, given their own histories, brought up their children as members of the middle class who had no doubt at all we were as privileged as anyone else. Though we had no money, the house was full of books of all sorts. My parents read to me practically from the moment I was born, and soon I was reading for myself.

I was, as I have said, aware that my mother's family had a long and fascinating, if not always distinguished, history. In my adulthood I traced my Grandfather Putnam's genealogy with some accuracy back to fourteenth century Puttenham, Penne, and Aston Abbots in Buckinghamshire, England. Mother was a direct descendant of Constable Carolina John Putnam of Salem Village, now Danvers, Massachusetts, who in 1692 was throwing the accused and hapless New England "witches" into jail, but *her* mother was a full-blooded Dane. Because the Putnams

— of Aston Abbots, Puttenham, and Penn in Buckinghamshire, England — were also originally Danes living in the Danelaw, my brother and I are actually as much Danish as Sicilian, which nobody believes.[1]

---

[1]See my book titled *Satan's Scourge: A Narrative of the Age of Witchcraft in England and New England 1580–1697* (Scottsdale: Star Cloud P, 2009), which is also a history of the Putnam family in Colonial America.

"MOM MAY"

My mother was always collecting pieces of junk and gimcracks. One of the earliest items in her hoard that I can recall was a bird in a raffia cage that jiggled and twittered when one wound it up. "Remember this?" she asked one day when I visited her on one of my leaves from the Navy. She went to a cupboard, opened the door, and pointed to the top shelf. "Can you get it down for me?"

I got a stool and handed her down the raffia cage. "Be careful now, it's very old." She took it and we both went to the table where she sat down and wound it up. It was an old toy; a yellow canary made of tin and cotton and feathers, with a bright orange beak, sat in the center of the cage. The base was tin, like a music box. A big wire key thrust out of its side. As she wound it the perch jerked and the bird went back and forth as it made several attempts to get started. When she had finished winding she put it on the table, and the bird began to bob and nod as its ratchet voice chirped out of springs and cogs.

After high school, while I was out sailing around the world on an aircraft carrier, the *USS Hornet,* my mother had begun signing her letters to me, "Mom May." It was an annoying pun, of a piece with her enjoying the music of Lawrence Welk and Liberace, collecting her gewgaws, and automatically bursting into tears if she couldn't get her way. My wife Jean early in our marriage discovered that tears turned me away from, not toward her, and I have seldom since seen her weep. When she does so now, I understand that something serious has occurred, but it took many years for me to overcome the aversion training mother inflicted upon her family.

Mother hadn't always been like that. Father had brought up the children of his sister, Vita Sardella, and they had a good deal of respect for their uncle's bride, "The Great Dane" as they called her when she came briefly to live with them, until I was born. But for five more years the two families continued to live in the same Buffalo, New York, neighborhood until, in 1939, we moved to Meriden, Connecticut, leaving my aunt and cousins behind. In particular my girl cousins, "Little" Josie ("Big" Josie was married to my cousin Joseph) and Sarah, tell stories of how, when they couldn't turn to their own old-country mother for information about such things as menstrual problems, my mother would show them how modern

American women had learned to cope. The cousins would always be grateful for mother's expertise in such matters and for her willingness to discuss them.

I did not know this woman myself. By the time I was old enough to begin forming coherent memories, mother was on her way to becoming a second-class citizen in the world and in the family. Father was partly to blame, for he was well into middle-age when he married and too set in the old-country attitudes toward women to change much. He wasn't cruel — there was never a less cruel man; he was just too wrapped up in his ministerial vocation to take notice of her. That was too much to bear for a woman who had hauled herself out of nineteenth-century, midwestern rural poverty by a sheer act of sustained willpower triggered by, evidently, a religious experience of some sort. It was also an insult to a trained missionary who felt she too had a calling to be something other than a parent:

She was thirty-five when I was born, set in her ways herself, independent, better educated than her husband, much more practical. When my father informed her — having himself led the life of a Lothario before he got religion and stopped sowing wild oats — that sex had only one purpose, procreation, and then followed that edict up with non-action, her sense of her worth must have plummeted into the pool of self-pity that she renewed with tears of frustration for most of the rest of her life. But of course I understood none of this until it was far too late to do anything, even if something could have been done.

Nevertheless, Mom May had always wanted to serve people. All she asked in return were continuing expressions and postures of gratitude. She wished to be surrounded by adoring crowds of Italian folk for whom she was willing to make great sacrifices, provided only that they understood her superior position. I don't believe she ever realized that everyone, including her two sons, could sense her essentially condescending nature, despite the good she certainly did for people.

Father, on the other hand, was willing to give his time, his strength, and even his limited money to the impoverished, the helpless, the troubled, and he did so without so much as a hint of anything but kindness and charity. As a result, everyone loved father, whose greatest failing was that he assumed everyone else saw things exactly as he did and was willing to do as much.

Almost no one liked mother, who was infuriated by the street people my father brought home from time to time to share our frugal Depression meals. Little Josie has told me that she and her siblings often went hungry, when father was living with them, because of this habit of her uncle. It seemed to them that it was always their rations and their mother's, not his, that were cut in order to make the meals stretch to cover the unwelcome strangers.

The first incident involving mother that I remember hearing about, and the one that set the tone of our entire life in Meriden, had to do with Miss Delphine Avery, the unmarried missionary lady who was attached to the First Italian Baptist Church, which father was selected to lead in 1939. Miss Avery, though she too was a Yankee, was well-liked by the church people. The tale as I heard it was that the congregation was not large enough to contain two trained missionaries, one of whom was the minister's wife. It was alleged that when father defended Miss Avery against Mom May's encroachments, he was accused of disloyalty and mother began to imagine that there was something going on between Papa and Miss Avery — there was assuredly nothing going on between Mom May and Papa, not until they agreed to give me a brother five years younger than I.

The folklore of the church holds that mother's forays against Miss Avery grew in bitterness and frequency, and eventually Miss Avery decided that she could do work elsewhere with more effect and less stress. Mom May stood triumphant — the parishioners maintain — among the wreckage of whatever career she had hoped to have in that church, and there are church people who still remember angrily, or so they believe, what mother did, though it is decades since father led the little flock of immigrants and a few other strayed sheep that he had managed to round up on the streets of the city.

It is a measurement of the degree to which the parish folk disliked my mother that this construction of events involving Miss Avery is completely false, according to the missionary herself. It is at this point that a series of coincidences begins: When I was a child, my father was a counselor for a year or two at Royal Ambassadors Boy's Camp at Ocean Park in Maine — I was a camper there myself. Ocean Park was, and it still is, an interdenominational summer enclave, with a weighting toward the Baptists, on the Maine coast near Saco, a mile below Old Orchard Beach. It is also the site of one of the oldest writers' conferences in the country, the State of Maine, co-founded by Adelbert Jakeman and my dear late friend, Loring Williams, who was largely responsible for the publication of my *First Poems* in 1960, and wholly responsible for the publication of my chapbook *The Sketches* two years later.

Another feature of Ocean Park is a retirement village for religious workers. When I was serving as poet-in-residence at the writers' conference during the summer of 1988, I was handed a message that Delphine Avery had been in the audience for one of my programs and wanted to say hello. It was too late for us to get together that summer, but I phoned her, and the next year Jean and I took her out to lunch where we got the true story from her.

Miss Avery said that missionaries are sent out to a place for a maximum period of two years, and after that they are automatically reassigned, because the Italian Baptist Association doesn't want any parish to grow too dependent on them. The missionary's job is to get things organized and running, and then to hand over the reins to the preacher. Unfortunately, my father came a year late to Meriden, so Delphine had stayed that extra year, and bonds that were perhaps too strong had developed between her and some of the parishioners — Delphine told us that day that some of the Meriden people still came to Ocean Park to visit her once or twice a year. She professed to know nothing of any problem between herself and Mom May. We had to believe her, and I'm grateful I had a chance to learn the true tale from one of the principals, but I now know more than I want to about the rumor-mongering that goes on in a Christian congregation.

Although mother wasn't tall, she was somewhat taller than papa who was about five-foot-five, I would surmise. She gave the impression that she was tall, though, because she was square-shouldered, she had good posture — which no doubt she had been taught in school, and she was sturdily built. People think that my own coloring — dark brown hair, brown eyes, ruddy complexion — must be ethnic, inherited from my father, but in fact that was my mother's coloring, for papa had jet black hair, gray eyes, and skin so fair that he and his similarly-colored sister Beatrice were called the "Prince" and "Princess" in Riesi, Sicily, when they were children.

Mother could do many things with her hands when she was called upon to do so, things like bookbinding and making costumes, that she had been taught in missionary school and were supposed to be put to use in Sunday school. Gradually, though, over the years, as she made more — and more intransigent — enemies, these skills grew rusty and finally deteriorated into mere file-keeping and album-arranging. Yet wherever we moved we carried with us relics and mementos of her past projects.

I would love to go up into the attic of whatever house we were living in at the time and poke around in the trunks. There I would find things like old suits of mail — made of silver-painted burlap left over from a church pageant Mom May had staged in some archaic year before history had begun with my birth. One Halloween when I was five or six years old, she let me wear Sir Galahad's costume, complete with cardboard shield and wooden sword, and I won a five dollar prize for it at the city contest in Columbus Park. When I was older and mother had lost interest in the old costumes, my friend Dicky Hass and I dueled with those swords in the driveway of the parsonage, the battles stopping only when the weapons fell apart or our thumbs got mashed.

As time windled along, Mom May was reduced among our parishioners and our neighbors — which included much of the town one way and another, for we moved nearly every year until the church purchased a parsonage — to the status of resident curmudgeon. When I was very young I recall vividly a handyman named Mr. Scully, when he had been called upon to erect a clothes pole at our house on Newton Street and had spent a long while listening to Mom May's blistering directions and criticisms, turning to me and saying, "I would do anything for your father, but for your mother . . . nothing!"

At last she had left only a single bosom friend, a nasty-tempered farm woman whom Gene and I called "Clara Cow." We would come home and find Clara sitting, with her rangy frame and broad, scowling face, in the living room drinking coffee and chatting with mother in a whiny, drawly voice. I recall Clara best in the house on South Avenue that my parents managed to buy from their landlady's sister — oddly enough, they had gotten along very well with their last landlady, and Mom May was genuinely sorry when she died. The sister, knowing they had been friends, sold mama and papa the house at an extremely reasonable price. These were the early years of my marriage, when Jean and I were living in Storrs, Connecticut, Iowa City, and Cleveland.

But it was in the earlier dwellings of my childhood that I really saw most of Clara, who had never been married. Although she lived on a farm, her father, as I recall, had been a judge. For some reason, Clara would take every opportunity to insult or belittle me, even when I was a child, and I assume she did the same to my brother Gene. When I was an adult, Clara would ask me about my first teaching job at Fenn College in Cleveland, and then point out how much more money her father made as a judge, and what a superior social position he occupied. I eventually got over being annoyed or angry with Clara and simply ignored her. At last even this final friendship dissolved, and my mother was left to fight with the neighbors.

For she had even alienated her younger son and his wife who, during the first years of their marriage, lived on the first floor of the South Avenue house, which the landlady had once occupied. Gene had gone into the Navy a year after I was discharged, and when he had completed his hitch he got a job and married — he had never been interested in going to college. While he and his family lived with our parents, after work and on weekends he labored to put the somewhat run-down and old-fashioned place into excellent order. For one thing, he tore out and dug up the dirt cellar and poured a concrete floor all by himself.

When Gene and Judy's first child, Stephen, was born, papa was overjoyed. He loved being able to play with and take care of the baby, but Mom May liked to order Judy around and tell her how badly she was raising her child. At last Judy made Gene buy their own home in Bristol, about twenty miles from Meriden, where Judy's family lived, and they moved out. The rift that existed between Judy and Mom May was never to be bridged.

After papa died Mom May participated in senior citizen activities. She took bus trips here and there, and she even went to Hawaii where she bought a small round plastic pseudo-aquarium with plastic fish swimming in it, but she eventually lost interest even in going to the various Meriden churches — any of them but my father's old place, by then known as the Grace Baptist and under the direction of a young non-Italian preacher. She was left to sit alone then in her living room looking out the windows at the neighbors who were always trying to get away with something. She had her gewgaws about her, and extras stashed in the closets and the attic to give away to anyone who might happen along and stumble into her dusty web. She had her Liberace records and the television set papa had been watching the night he pitched forward into death.

One day I drove down to Meriden from Oswego, New York, to visit and take Mom May to a reading of my poetry that I had been invited to present in New York City. I had used to stay in an attic room at the South Avenue place — actually, a finished room in the unfinished third floor of the house — but mother wanted me to sleep on a couch in the living room because she'd not "had the time" to clean upstairs. She'd also not had the time to clean downstairs, or to buy food for herself, let alone me, to eat. I took her out for dinner.

In the middle of the night the antique couch collapsed and I awoke in distress and confusion, choking in an explosion of dust bunnies. The next morning I found there was not even coffee in the house for breakfast. Mom May enjoyed New York at noon of a bright, sunny day, where I read in Battery Park among a listless smore of noon lunchers and a few poets and friends. On my way back to Oswego I stopped at Gene's and told him mother could no longer take care of herself. Though he had been visiting her regularly, he hadn't noticed that she became disoriented and sometimes didn't know where she was after getting out of a car in front of her own home, was not eating right if at all, never changed or washed her clothes, didn't clean the house. It had all happened too gradually, I guess, but when I pointed out the facts, he recognized their reality.

The last time we all — both families — took Mom May out, we went for a walk in Hubbard Park in Meriden. But it was the year when the spruce budworms were devouring New England, and they hung from the park trees on their long filaments, crawled over the skeletal leaves of the trees and dropped excrement on our heads, or fell themselves down our collars. We walked on their bodies. We went shopping, then to lunch. Mother wore a men's crew-neck T-shirt under her blouse, and it was yellow. It was difficult to sit next to her, breathe normally, and eat at the same time.

Gene made arrangements, with my consent, to put Mom May into a retirement home near him just outside Bristol, and there she stayed for several years, fading into silence, paying little attention to what went on around her. She broke her hip and would no longer get out of bed. And one day, when she had long-since forgotten how to cry and no longer cared for anything at all that went on in the world, she died.

We buried her next to the ashes of our father in Walnut Grove Cemetery in Meriden. We were solemn, but there were no tears except for those of Jean's and my high-school friend, Marie. She had recently lost her own widowed mother, with whom she had lived in her childhood home for several years after divorce, and of whom she had complained most of her life. Now, she found that she could weep for us all. "It's so much harder than I thought it would be," she said.

When I think back I remember Mom May best in the summertime, on an evening heavy with heat that wrapped the parsonage on Windsor Avenue in its smothering arms. As I stare out of the window of the bedroom I share with my brother Gene, a crisp breeze comes walking down the row of thick elms that stop abruptly at the corner where the Italian neighborhood starts. The breeze seems like a breath of September. It is cool. It clears my nostrils and smells fresh. It darkens my blues. Fall has always been a melancholy season, I recall, but fall in June is nearly unbearable. I rise to go downstairs.

Mother is in the kitchen. I walk past her, out the screen door, letting it slam behind me on its spring. "Where are you going?" she asks. "It's late to be going out, isn't it?"

I look at her through the dusty mesh — she is perspiring and dabbing her face with a soggy handkerchief. She is sitting at the table. A plate of what had been ice-cream is at her elbow. She faces away from it toward me. Her hair is still solid brown, though she is well into middle age, and she looks as oaken as the trees her father had felled to build the Wisconsin farmstead which, once sown, had sprung to seed at once.

"I'll be back in a while. It's hot. It ought to be nice driving." I start down the back steps. "Want to come?"

She shakes her head. I leave her and the clock humming above the range to revolve the summer slowly in silence. I go out to the smashed pear tree dying beside the house; my '40 Chevy jalopy is parked under its wickety limbs, and I get in, start it. I back out of the drive.

Soon I am clattering along the roads at the western edge of town. The furtive moon rearrives and shines through the windshield; the clouds lift and there are stars. The hills around town pull me in and I drive up through Hubbard Park to Castle Craig, a tower some rich man long ago had built on East Peak, the little crop of rocks no large state would dare to call mountains. Castle Craig belongs to the city now, and I mount its black throat to come out again into the night. I look down on the place where I've grown up.

In the cool night the breeze is edgy and surreptitious among the leaves of the woods below. I stand and watch the lights out there, downward past Mirror Lake reservoir. And as I look, seeing the ripples of darkness glimmer and fade in the water and in the streets and yards of Meriden, it seems as though my blues have been dipped into the basin of understanding and come out pure. I know, for this brief space of clear time, the difference between sadness and guilt, between self-pity and scorn.

TO SMOKE A PIPE

Reading some Faulkner articles one day in a 2002 issue of *Pipes and Tobaccos*, which is edited by one of my former students, I was reminded of my own first purchase of a pipe and tobacco. One day when I was a kid my mother caught me in the bathroom of the parsonage smoking corn silk in a pipe I had hollowed out of a horse chestnut. I don't recall what I used for a stem.

Mom May was quite upset, of course, and she tried to extract from me a promise that I'd never smoke again. I wasn't willing to go that far; however, I promised her that I wouldn't smoke until my sixteenth birthday, and I kept that promise. But on May 2, 1950 — my sixteenth natal celebration — I went down to Whelan's drug store on the corner of Colony Street and West Main in Meriden. I looked over their stock, selected a Yello-Bole that looked exactly like a horse chestnut, and a can of Holiday Pipe Tobacco.

After my purchase I went home, sat on the back stoop, filled my new pipe and lit it. I was puffing away when my mother opened the back door, saw what I was doing, and went back inside, closing the screen door quietly. That was it. She didn't argue with me about it. I'd kept my promise, and that was all she could ask. A number of years later I wrote this poem which was originally titled "To Smoke a Pipe," but that I changed in order to include it in my collection titled, *The Compleat Melancholick*:

A MEDICINE FOR MELANCHOLY

Tobacco divine, rare, superexcellent Tobacco, which goes far beyond all their panaceas, potable gold, and philosopher's stones, a sovereign remedy to all diseases. — Burton.

  It ought to be a large old knot hole,
first of all, surrounded by most of the tree.
        Black inside, as though Hell had poked
        a smokestack out between your teeth.

  Now, heave a wheeze downstem hard until
you've blown a beachful of igneous grains out

into the bowl's bayou. Knock them
onto your palm. Whistle them off

like a ruinous wind. The carpet
will thrive, grow lush as Virginia. Sit back.
Knuckle off the roof of your root
cellar where your tobacco, as

loamy as moss, masses and awaits
a spark's attack. Thumb up a balesworth; trammel
it down deep into the devil's
eye. Snatch up an eruption now

and spang! Puff a belly full of fumes.
Whoof! Off go angels and satyrs; clouds of them —
furry thighs and messes of wings
bearing you off like an orgy.

I no longer smoke, haven't done so for decades, but I didn't quit smoking a pipe because I had stopped enjoying it. In fact, I still have that original Yello-Bole, and many another of my old collection, including the carved brier of Romulus and Remus that I bought in Rome while my ship, the *USS Hornet* was in Italy. Along the bottom of the bowl there was engraved the legend, "R-Roma," a fine pun and one that reminds me to this day of the thing I liked best about smoking.

THE MUTABLE PAST

The vacant lot where we North Third Street kids played softball on those sunny New England summer days was full of trees, and it was small. When we wanted to play hardball we went down the street, to West Main, crossed, walked a hundred feet or so to our left, and turned into the Lincoln Junior High School driveway. The school had a big playing field, but we were likely there to run into other young folk from adjacent neighborhoods, so we tended to stay within a two-block radius of our homes.

We were quite a crowd, mostly of an age. Bob Strauss lived across the street from me. He was a couple of years older, and he was practicing to become the New England fife-and-drum corps snare drum champion in a few years. Next door to him lived Phil Reilly who, like me, was in the sixth grade, but in parochial rather than public school. Down the street were the Gaffney brothers, Marty and Billy, a couple of tough, skinny kids, and across from them lived the Muravnick sisters, Janice and Pat. Janice played ball with us sometimes, for she was a tomboy. On Second Street there were the Carlson brothers, a couple of hard cases in my opinion, but I never really had trouble with them, though I recall worrying about it a good deal. Kenny Noack lived on the corner between my house and the vacant lot. Just at the edge of the lot there stood a mysterious shack. It appeared to have been a store because it had plate-glass windows, but one made out shapes through them with difficulty, they were so covered with grit.

When we had finished playing our game among the trees that were our bases and that turned the contest into an object lesson in ricochet physics, we would gather up our gear, such as it was — a ball, a bat or two, but hardly ever a glove — and head for home. On the way we might stop to peer in through the windows of the shack, the sun at our backs glinting off the dark glass. We would push our faces up as close as we could and use both hands to shield our eyes. Even so, all we could make out inside were the outlines of what appeared to be some machines.

Before we left we would rattle the padlock on the splinter-dry front door and speculate. Some of our guesses were fantastic, others more mundane. One theorized that the shack might be a rendezvous for spies — the Second World War had not long been over — who came only at night. Or it was an old machine shop left over from the war when many of our parents had been engaged in carrying two jobs at the same time in little war industries that had sprung up everywhere. Then our interest ebbed, and we forgot to think about it.

One summer after school had let out for good I took to getting up early — who knows why? — and hanging around the street while my slugabed friends kept their dreams alive. I recall one morning when I walked out the front door onto the big front porch, down the wooden stairs, then down the flight of concrete steps to the sidewalk, for our house sat up on a bank. I stood with my hands in my pocket, my eyes drinking in the early cool beneath the elms that used to line our avenues, sunlight mottling the road like the design of a Moorish carpet. I looked down the street, then up the street, and I spotted a battered prewar pickup truck sitting at the curb in front of the old shack. I noticed that the awning was down, something I hadn't seen before, and then from the doorway there emerged a man carrying a couple of what appeared to be boxes. He ducked under the awning, lifted his burden over the tailgate, arranged them, then turned and went back in.

Naturally, I sauntered up the block as quickly as possible without, I hoped, appearing to hurry, and soon I was standing where I could see inside. I could hear the machines running. When my eyes adjusted to the inner dusk, I saw the man — he was a big man — lifting milk cans and pouring their contents into a hopper. The machine rattled and ratcheted, bottles clattered as they were filled with white, foamy milk. The man was busy, for he was handling all the manual chores including putting bottles onto the conveyer belt, taking them off at the other end, and racking them in the crates. I waited until I was sure the milkman had seen me, then imperceptibly I edged closer to the center of action.

I don't recall how near I managed to get the first day, or the second, or even exactly when he spoke to me, but eventually I did get the idea he had no objection to my being there, or even to my lending a hand, such as it was, upon occasion. In fact, rather than words I recall mainly a friendly silence between us. I do remember that finally he asked me if I'd like to go out on his route with him, and I said yes. "Go ask your mom if it's all right," he said, and I did.

For some reason my mother agreed. She came down and spoke with him, but she must also have done some checking when I told her about the big man bottling milk in the mornings, and perhaps it was even she who told me the man's name was Walsh. At any rate, there came the morning when I helped Mr. Walsh load up and got into the seat beside him. Soon we were rattling around on the outskirts of town towards Wallingford and Yalesville — the bottles rattled with the old pickup, and our teeth did likewise, for there was little left of the suspension and nothing of the shock absorbers, if we had any.

The mornings passed pleasantly. We would go to the side or back door of a house to leave one or two or three of those old-fashioned round, long-necked bottles on the stoop. The cream would have risen to the top pretty well by the time we'd delivered the milk, and I could imagine the people in the house doing what my mother did, that is, carefully pouring some off the top into a morning cup of coffee. Before I drank a glass of such milk at home or poured it onto my cereal I would always shake the bottle to distribute the cream. Now I can't drink milk at all, not even the processed sort, for I can't digest it — nor can most adults, though not many people seem to know it. I should have realized this sooner because Bernie Jurale, my high school chemistry and home room teacher, kept telling us over and over that it was so. We students thought he was a crank, and that's why, when I developed an ulcer during my Navy days after high school, I drank lots of milk because doctors said it was good for the condition. How can doctors be so wrong so often? It was the worst thing they could have prescribed. Back in the 1940s, however, who knew these things? What I remember is the creamy, delicious taste of whole milk and, in the winter, the bottles of milk standing outside the back door with their caps raised into the air on a column of cream, for as the bottle froze its contents expanded. That's a sight no child will see again; these days, if people drink milk at all, skim milk, for milkfat is supposed to be bad for our cholesterol levels. Back then you got skim milk by skimming off all of the head of cream, but the resulting liquid tasted like blue chalk water, and it still does.

Sometimes one of our customers would open the door as we were making our delivery — a woman in a housecoat or a man dressed for work but without his jacket on. They might say, "Hello, Mr. Walsh," or "Good morning," and call my friend by his first name — was it Ed? Jim? And he would nod and smile. Then we'd get back into the truck and be on our way. When we had finished the route it would still be early. My friends would just be getting up and coming outdoors. Bob or Phil might see me waving to Mr. Walsh as he drove away. Soon we would begin our long summer day of ball or exploring or playing war or cops and robbers.

It was in 1959, when my wife and I were living in Storrs, Connecticut, and I was attending the university there that my mother sent me the newspaper obituary of a local man named "Big Ed" Walsh. Mom May was always sending me clippings from the local papers — I'd left a paper trail of her gleanings completely around the world, for she had kept me apprised of local affairs all the while I had been in the Navy — through boot camp in Maryland, my first assignment in Norman, Oklahoma, the two years I'd spent aboard the aircraft carrier *Hornet* while she circled the globe, and my fourth year as a Yeoman in Arlington, Virginia, at the Bureau of Naval Personnel where I became the most famous and mythical of sailors, the fellow who sat on the shore duty list.

I don't know what led me to believe that the subject of the obituary was my milkman friend. Was it something my mother wrote in her letter? I can't find it in my files. Was it the picture that ran with the death notice? Was it merely a conclusion that I'd jumped to? I'd had some suspicions before then that Mr. Walsh had been a ballplayer, but in my childhood I was, and am still, a pure Yankee fan. I knew little or nothing of any other team except the Yankees' archrival Boston Red Sox.

Oh, I'd had an experience with the Philadelphia Athletics who'd come to town to play an exhibition game with our semi-pro Insilco team at Insilco Field (now a shopping mall) sponsored by the International Silver Company that gave our town, Meriden, the sobriquet "Silver City." If I'm not mistaken, Connie Mack had once managed the Meriden team. I went to that game on the day that had been named for him, and I saw Mr. Mack with my own eyes, but I was not otherwise one of the cognoscenti of the ballpark. Whatever it was, something convinced me that I'd been delivering milk in Connecticut with Big Ed Walsh, a Hall-of-Fame player for the Chicago White Sox from 1904 to 1916, and a one-season forty-game winner at a time when giants bestrode the mound and raced around the diamond track. Big Ed had been born in 1881, so when we were both residents of the same town he was about sixty-five years of age. He'd spent one year, 1917, with the Boston National League team before he retired at the age of thirty-six. He had thus been doing other things for twenty-nine years before I rode my summer milk route with my friend.

I've been living in Central New York State for many years, now, and ten or twelve years back I drove down to Cooperstown with another elderly friend, Charlie Davis, who had been a jazz-band leader during the years of Ed Walsh's early retirement. I used to get a bang out of thinking that Ed must have heard Charlie's famous jazz composition "Copenhagen" many times on his crystal set. Charlie and I went winding down through the hills and picnicked in a lakeside park there in Cooperstown. We attended a meeting of the New York State Folklore Association where Charlie was a featured speaker, having turned into a writer and publisher in one of his several incarnations. And then we went over to the Baseball

Hall of Fame where I looked up Big Ed.

There he was, on the wall with the other titans of bat and mound. I tried to get into a suitable mood of awe as I stood there, but had no success at it. All I could see reflected in what I perceived to be memory's lake was a dusty road unwinding before the beat-up hood of an old pickup, and a bottle of milk that wore a crown of cream. Later, I wrote a prize-winning poem about those summer mornings and my friend, Mr. Walsh, and later still I did a short nostalgic piece for a national magazine which brought me letters and phone calls from all sorts of people who remembered Big Ed Walsh and the Meriden of my childhood as vividly as I did. Jim Masterson, a high school classmate, phoned to chat about it, and so did our choral director at M. H. S., Tony Parisi, but we weren't at home for his call so my son, Christopher, took the message and relayed it to Maine where we were vacationing.

John P. Kiley, Sr., wrote from Derby, Connecticut. "I organized and was chairman of the Naugatuck Valley Old Time Athletes," he informed me. "We were fortunate to have Big Ed as the featured speaker both in 1950 and 1951. The Hotel Clark (since razed) in Derby was filled to the walls because Big Ed was coming and all the Old Timers (some in their 80s . . .) had a chance to meet, listen to, and shake hands with him. As the chairman I can say it was one of the happiest occasions. I still have scrap books of the events and will pass them on to my son and grandsons. I am eighty-eight, so I remember the Chicago White Sox when we listened on ticker tape or radio. I have pitching tips written by Big Ed and also his autograph."

Another who responded was Warren F. Gardner, who was Editor of *The Morning Record* of Meriden for many years, including that couple of years when I worked as high school correspondent for the paper and as cub reporter and morgue clerk as well (the "morgue" is the file of clippings on people and events that all newspapers maintain). Warren wrote, "I was delighted to read your little piece about Big Ed Walsh. . . . You were lucky to know him. I knew he was a baseball player of repute, but until I read your column I did not know that he ran the dairy on North Third Street.

"I remember the dairy well, of course. I was born in 1909 in the second floor apartment of the house at 45 North Fourth Street. Father owned the house. He rented the downstairs apartment. We lived there until I was age 16, then moved to Carpenter Avenue.

"So I grew up on the West Side and loved it. We had good neighbors; I can remember many of them. We had milk delivered to our back door in the glass bottles you mentioned. No such thing as homogenizing in those days, either of milk or men.

"On occasion, if we ran short of milk or mother wanted some cream, I was sent to get it at Walsh's dairy, often bringing it home in the small pail I carried with me. Whoever waited on me dipped it out of the vat. In those days milkmen made deliveries by horse and wagon. There was a barn in the rear of the little milk station where the horse was stabled. On one occasion my father sprained his wrist badly while trying to crank the open Ford Model T touring car we had. Dr. E. W. Smith advised a poultice made of hay seeds soaked in hot water and wrapped around the wrist. Where to get hay seeds? Mr. Walsh's hay loft, of course. So father and I went there, and with Walsh's permission scooped up about a pint of seeds from the bottom of the mow."

But the nostalgia piece that Warren Gardner and John Kiley read and responded to also brought me a letter from a man now living in Massachusetts, Raymond E. Burke, who said that, although many things in my essay were accurate, the central fact was not a fact at all, for I had confused Big Ed Walsh with another man named Walsh, proprietor for many years of Walsh's Dairy on North Third Street. Mr. Burke wrote that "The man that ran J. J. Walsh Dairy was James J. Walsh . . . and [his] home was on Columbus Avenue." According to him, by 1949 the dairy no longer existed because it was ". . . closed and Walsh sold his milk route to another milk dealer . . . in the middle '40s." How can the past transform itself like that? How can one remember things that never existed? For I did a lot of checking, particularly through Warren Gardner, and discovered that Mr. Burke was correct. Warren wrote, "It looks like a case of mistaken identity. Today I checked several Meriden city directories from about 1930 to 1950. The earlier directories gave no occupation for Edward A. Walsh, merely his home address, until 1950 when the listing read: 'Edward A. Walsh, caretaker Broad Brook reservoir h[ome] Finch av[enue] bey[ond] town line.'"

I recall that the obituary my mother sent me had mentioned that Big Ed was the caretaker of a reservoir in Meriden, and Mr. Burke said that he and his father had struck up an acquaintance with the former baseball great when they went fishing there. The obituary never mentioned a milk route, but I had nevertheless been convinced somehow that my summer morning companion had been a retired ball-player.

In one of my forays back to my home town I had myself acquired a copy of *The Meriden Directory*, vol. 73 for 1949. I have it before me now, and under "W" it has exactly the entries that Warren Gardner quoted, and it has no listing for the dairy itself, thus confirming Mr. Burke's claim that by then it had been sold. Warren tried to make me feel better about my error. He wrote, "I have no doubt whatsoever that you believed the man you helped deliver milk was 'Big Ed' himself. As a boy I delivered the *Morning Record* to a Pilkington family at the east end of North Avenue. Charlie Pilkington, a young son in the family, was in the news as a promising young amateur prize fighter. He and Kid Kaplan, who went on to win the world's championship for his weight, were contemporaries. I always hoped that Charlie, who was a hero in the neighborhood, at least among the boys, would answer the door when I collected for the paper, but he never did, and I never saw him. I never saw 'Big Ed' Walsh either."

THE HUSTLE

One weekend while I was in the Navy and my brother Gene was in high school I came back on liberty to Meriden and discovered that he had gotten himself into some sort of trouble. Papa and Mom May talked to me about it in distress, and I think I must have become angry, because I wrote this poem:

O your eyes are slightly wondered,
    Brother Gene.
They allow the world's been sundered,
    Brother Gene.
So you travel with your brothers:
Not the flesh-and-blood kind — others
Who deplore the ways of fathers,
    Man! you're mean.

There are rods and there are women,
    Brother Gene.
You're a rebel, you're a demon,
    Brother Gene.
You were spawned beneath the atom
On a lower social stratum.
People stink, and so you hate 'em,
    Bile and spleen.

What's a lifetime's secret essence,
    Brother Gene?
Is it kooky adolescence,
    Brother Gene?
Is it ninety miles per hour,
Is it acting beat and dour,
Or professionally sour?
    Cool the scene.

We will halve the world and share it,
    Brother Gene.
Call half minah, call half parrot,
    Brother Gene.

In our monstrous aviaries
We will ostracize canaries . . .,
Any bird that sings or varies
In between.

Then we'll blow the whole bit higher,
Brother Gene,
Than the sun shoots tongues of fire,
Brother Gene.
For commitment's too much trouble;
Prick the big dream like a bubble.
You can be the final rebel,
Brother Gene.

It was very strange, it seemed to me, that Gene had gotten into a scrape because he was, and still is in 2008, a very nice guy. He had never been a minute's trouble all his childhood, to my recollection, though I was pretty mean to him out of sibling rivalry, I suppose. Still, for most of our lives we have gotten along pretty well, our wives like each other, and our kids all get along on those few occasions when they get together. The poem is an over-reach, over-the-top. Reading it now, it seems to me that I was writing about the 1950s, not my brother.

Jean and I had graduated from Meriden High in 1952. By three years later rock-n-roll had arrived, the new teen-agers were acting quite strangely, wearing d. a. hairdos (that's "duck's ass" in case anyone wonders) and developing the culture that would eventually lead to *American Graffiti* and *Hair* and James Dean's *Rebel without a Cause*. My wife and I had grown up in the post-World War II culture, where the last days of swing and bebop and bobbysox were fading into the unsettling and ominous future.

GENE AND GENES

The small, white-clapboarded First Italian Baptist Church of Meriden, Connecticut, was located at the edge of the Italian section of the city on Springdale Avenue. Here and there in the neighborhood a business would be run by one of my father's parishioners, but most of the shops with which we dealt were owned by members of the community majority. As far as many of our neighbors were concerned, my brother Gene and I were the sons of a "priest."

Now and then father's sister, Aunty Vita Sardella, would come down for a visit from Buffalo where I had been born and father had begun his clerical career. She would always bring some of our cousins, Joseph and Salvatore, Josephine and Sarah — the young women had baby-sat me when I was a toddler, but Sal was my favorite. They were all Protestants too, converted in this country not long after my father and his sister had immigrated. Gene, who was five years younger than I and had never lived in Buffalo, was more or less a stranger to the Sardella family.

Gene and I are a mixed breed both ethnically and religiously. When I was five years of age, my brother was born in Meriden. His middle name is "Laurent" — probably the female version of "Laura," my mother's middle name; it was many years before I realized the derivation of "Gene": it is the American version of "Gino," which is short for "Luigi" — my father had named both his sons after himself, even though neither of us is actually named "Luigi"!

It was not until we were seven and twelve years of age respectively that Gene and I learned about mother's people. During the summer of 1946 mother took us on our first and only trip to visit her family in the Middle West, where she had been raised. "Mom May," as she took to signing her letters toward the end of her life, had been born in Wayne, Nebraska, on May Day, 1899, the third of nine children — including six sons and three daughters — in the family of William Herbert Putnam, eighty-nine that year; his second wife, Laura Christina Larsen Putnam, was seventy-two, the mother — so far as we know — of all his children, though he had been married previously. The family had moved to Superior, Wisconsin, during mother's childhood, and all her family were still living in that area with the exception of her sister Lillian, who had died young.

I was old enough to have begun to understand that our family was very poor. When father died I saw some of his old tax records and documents, and as a

Baptist preacher he had never made more than $2500.00 a year in his life. Still, my brother and I were raised as though we were members of the middle class, and our expectations were middle class expectations — there is a great deal to be said, it seems to me, for the way in which people *think* of themselves, as distinguished from their actual financial situation. When we got to Superior I saw what real poverty was all about.

The Putnam homestead was a large oblong shack of two storeys standing near a barn which, it seems to me looking back over this cairn of years, was in better shape than the house whose weathered clapboards showed no sign of having been painted during modern times. Indoors, the floor undulated in great waves of worn wood. I don't believe there was a cellar underneath the building. Certainly there was no insulation, for there were no plaster walls. The only thing between the inner and outer climates was the sheathing of pine. In fact, it was nothing more than a barn itself.

The house was heated by a large free-standing wood stove in the middle room, and by a wood-burning cast iron cookstove in the kitchen where the zinc sink had no faucets, only a hand pump. There was no other indoor plumbing. Instead, Gene and I were introduced for the first time in our lives to privy facilities. I for one was glad we were visiting in midsummer rather than winter, though the yellowjackets and wasps that called the out-house home were something of a concern.

In the house an unenclosed stairway rose to the second floor where the bedrooms were located. We must have stayed in one or two of them, but I have no recollection of having done so. I do remember finding a large stone filled with amethysts on the stairs. I admired it so much that Grandma gave it to me, and I brought it back to Meriden where I added it to the bookcase museum I had in the bedroom Gene and I shared in the parsonage.

I have but one clear memory of Grandpa, a lean old man with a stubble beard who didn't bother with the privy for certain necessities if it weren't convenient. I had gone out into the yard and was wandering about the place when I caught him standing up against the outside wall of the barn relieving himself, giving the sere planks a good soaking. When he caught sight of me he buttoned himself up and disappeared like smoke into a breeze. I seldom spotted him after that, and always only at a distance.

Grandma was much more in evidence during our visit. I have no recollection of hearing her speak, though she must have done so, of course. She was a pure second-generation Danish-American, born in Manistee, Michigan, of parents who had immigrated from Denmark. It is this fact that led my Sicilian relatives in Buffalo to refer to my mother as "The great Dane." There was both affection and disdain in that pun.

Grandma's demeanor was always grim. She had no sense of humor, so far as I could tell — no more than mother had. She always wore an apron, whether in or out of the house; she was always busy cooking or cleaning or darning socks and had little time for a prepubescent grandson. Still, for some reason I fell in love with her and I liked to go with her when she had to attend to errands or chores.

Despite the fact that the homestead was called a "farm," it had no land other than that on which the buildings stood, so Grandma's garden plot was located in a vacant lot several blocks away. Each day when she went to gather raspberries or vegetables I went with her to help and to carry some of the things back to the house. On the way we stopped at least once at a corner store where they sold ice cream cones dipped to order in various candy sprinkles. I can taste the colors still.

Our uncles were all very large men, generally affable and easy-going. None of them still lived on the homestead. Gene and I had two favorites — Uncle Arny and, our absolute favorite, Uncle Ed, who worked in a steel mill and stood well over six feet tall. We still own a snapshot of him with Gene, me, and his two sons draped all over him as he stands grinning into the camera.

Family legend has it that a young man at the steel mill once decided that he wanted to make his mark and chose to try to pick a fight with the biggest man around, Ed Putnam. Uncle Ed ignored him or brushed off his sallies and insults for a time, which only infuriated the young man more. At last he took a swing at Ed who didn't bother to swing back, but merely caught the approaching fist in his own hand and began to squeeze and bend the young fellow's wrist back. When at last the attacker was kneeling on the floor at Uncle Ed's feet, gritting his teeth in pain, Ed suggested that an apology was in order and a cessation of hostilities. He got both and there was no more trouble between them.

When we visited the farm of Uncle Arthur Bakken — who had married Aunt Myrtle, four years older than mother — he took Gene and me fishing at a lake nearby. Gene caught eight fish off one side of the boat, and I caught three off the other. When I insisted on trading sides, Gene caught five more, but I caught only four. On another occasion all the men and boys were bringing in hay on a flat-bed, open-slat, horse-drawn wagon. I was allowed to drive the wagon and was doing a good and prideful job of it when I stepped slightly to one side. My leg slipped down between the slats, which were covered with a thin layer of hay, and I was caught solid, held by the boards clear up to my crotch. I had the most enormous, purple-yellow bruise the full length of my thigh, but the thing that hurt worst was my failure as a driver. Clearly, life had it in for me.

Of the brothers only Harvey, born in 1897, was older than mother. Arnold was next in line, born in 1900, and Ed was third youngest, born in 1906. Of them all, May was the only one who managed to pull herself away from Wisconsin-Minnesota and attend college. She went to Chicago where she enrolled in secretarial school and became a stenographer during the heyday of the famous mobsters. She told us that one of them was gunned down on the street where she lived, almost beneath her window.

Where and when she got religion I do not know, but it was her ambition to become a missionary. She migrated east and managed, working as a secretary, to put herself through the School of Religious Education of Boston University where she took her bachelor's degree. Afterward she began to do work among the Italian immigrants near Wakefield, Massachusetts, and it was there that she met father, who had converted to Protestantism and started on the road to becoming a minister.

One of Mom May's legacies to me were two albums filled with pictures, documents, letters, and memorabilia of various kinds, all of these arranged in chronological order. The most interesting item in them, to me, is this letter written on letterhead of the Colgate-Rochester Divinity School and datelined "December 19, 1932":

> Dear Miss Putnam,
>
> I know that you do not welcome my correspondence, but that does not matter. I do not like to reciprocate the same attitude, or in other words: I do not want to act according to the Old Testament procedure, namely, eye for eye, tooth for tooth. I like to think of you, gently, of those beautiful days of Christian friendship which we spent together in that Methodist Camp, and once [a] year, at least, I want to share it to you by sending to you a Christmas card.
>
> This year is a special Christmas for me, therefore, I am accompanying my Christmas card with this letter. The speciality consists that the second Sunday of December I began a new work in Buffalo. At the corner of Rhode Island and Normal Ave. there is a beautiful American church. It is a modern building of bricks, and it [is] surrounded by 40,000 Italians. All the American people have almost moved elsewhere, and the Buffalo Baptist Union decided to begin our Italian mission. The English meetings still continue, but in addition to them I began the work in Italian. the American minister is still there, of course, who carries the

work in English. The time will come when that church will fall completely in the hands of the Italians. Then I shall be happy to be at the head of two big churches. In the morning now I am preaching in my old church, the Second Italian Baptist Church, in which I enjoy to preach to a congregation of more than one hundred individuals, in the afternoon I preach in this new church; last Sunday I had 17 persons. It is very good at the beginning. I feel now that God has called me to do an outstanding piece of work here in Buffalo where we have a colony of 75,000 Italians.

As far as school is concerned this is my last year of my theological course; I need only 28 hours of credit to finish my college work. It is almost another year of work then I shall be glad to be thru [*sic*] and receive my two degrees. This will give me a great confidence and courage in thinking that my education is not inferior to certain Italian and American pastors who look down at the poor missionaries who have not a college and seminary education.

You may question now to yourself, "Why is Mr. Turco telling to me that?" The answer will be this: because my heart is full of joy and I need some one to manifest this joy, and I selected you, this time, to be the recipient to pour the joy of my heart. Do you not appreciate it?

Cordially yours,
L. Turco

When our parents were married the following year, mother was already thirty-four years of age and father was forty-three. I have believed for years that they ought not to have gotten together. It was a disaster for her, for it brought to an end the long process of her turning herself into something extraordinary. Not that father was in any way unkind — I can hardly imagine a more compassionate man, but his upbringing in the old country had been typical. He was the man of the house, it was his calling that came first, and mother necessarily came second. It was more than she could bear, and she died a very unhappy and unfulfilled woman.

Life, however, is full of paradoxes. Mother and father had found it necessary to take industrial jobs during the second world war. Afterward mother kept working, though as a stenographer, not a production-line worker, and father became the homemaker and housekeeper, because his vocation kept him around the house most of the time. This sort of thing did not happen in the rest of America until after the "Women's Liberation" movement of the nineteen-sixties.

When Mom May came to Massachusetts from Chicago she was returning to her roots. According to the family genealogy, *The Putnam Lineage* by Eben Putnam, published in Salem when Mom May was eight years old, the Putnam family, in the persons of John Putnam, his wife and sons, had settled in Salem by 1639 or 1640. I had been aware of the family link with the Salem trials in a vague way as early as high school. Some of my first writing was on the subject, of which Mom May disapproved, for during my junior year at Meriden High I wrote a "Witch Trial" script for Senior Skit Night in 1951. Our club, The Fantaseers, performed it to vast local acclaim. There is a photograph of it in my book *Fantaseers, A Book of Memories.*

The year before, I had written in Doc Michel's sophomore English class an addendum — a final chapter imitating Nathaniel Hawthorne's style — to *The House of the Seven Gables.*[1] I kept wondering about Salem, however, so in middle age I researched and wrote a 1200-page manuscript, *Satan's Scourge, A Narrative of the Age of Witchcraft in England and New England 1580–1697.* It was still unpublished in 2008, but researching it and writing it gave me more information than I really needed about the Putnams of America, nearly all of whom are descended from one immigrant family.

Scourge is a book of history, a chronicle of the period when the Age of Sympathetic Magic, which had been the system by which mankind operated from time immemorial, was beginning to shift over to the Age of Science, "The New Philosophy," by which the world would be increasingly governed from then forward. The main focus of the book is upon the Putnam family of Buckinghamshire, in England, from the birth of John Putnam, born in 1580, some of whose descendants would be deeply involved in the last gasp of sympathetic magic, the great witchcraft explosion of Salem Village, Massachusetts, in 1692, which is the climax of the book.

The volume not only looks at *all* the witchcraft cases in England and New England during the period covered, but it also tells the stories of the major scientists and Adepts of sympathetic magic (often the two were the same) in Europe and America. The effect is twofold: First, the method is strictly chronological, unfolding like a tapestry year by year. As one thread of the tapestry swells and tapers off, others appear and interweave with one another. Second, the history is told from the point of view of common people, the Puritans of England and New England primarily, but also the crystal gazers, alchemists, alleged witches and their accusers, and those ordinary citizens caught up in the webs woven by plotters, liars, "possessed" children — including the "witch bitch" Annie Putnam — and their parents, and, of course, the clerics.

Furthermore, this is the period when America was settled, when Oliver

[1]"The Great Collapse," published for the first time on-line in *Nights and Weekends*.com e-zine on March 21, 2009.

Cromwell and the Roundheads carried out their Puritan revolution, and all the politics and machinations of the relevant sovereigns and courtiers of the period are also a part of the tapestry woven.

When she was younger, my mother wrote also. I have found copies of some of her religiously-oriented stories in the meticulous secretarial files she kept on everyone throughout her life. In those same files I have found many of my own early attempts to write, most of them stories of science fiction or the supernatural. To judge from these facts one might surmise that there are two genetic traits that have continued down through the years of the lineage: first, a strong religious streak that takes some strange twists and, second, an equally strong literary bent that arises among the Putnams from time to time despite the environment, for there are many members of the family who are publishers, librarians, and writers including my daughter, Melora, who is a librarian. An even greater number, however, are artisans, laborers, soldiers and farmers. My brother Gene is a toolmaker, and I am a writer. It's a curious heritage.

My mother was the only one of the Putnam siblings to exhibit the literary and religious traits both, and she passed them on to me, except that in my case the religious bent was bent backwards. I continue to write fantasies, although I have spent years trying to break myself of the habit, but fortunately "magical realism" is currently a popular and respectable type of fiction. However, I lost my religion — if ever I had it truly — about the same time as our trip to Wisconsin.

Mother took Gene and me to a beach on one of Wisconsin's many beautiful lakes. I recall another child's body flung up on the sand, its flesh blue, a pallid blue. Gene saw the child also, as he has told me in recent years. Though I've thought of the accident often over the decades, I didn't discuss it with anyone until after mother's death, not even Gene.

One day after we had gotten back to Meriden from that trip to Wisconsin I experienced a revelation — I felt I was absolutely in this physical world where I did not particularly want to be. It was clear in that moment of enlightenment that one had to make the best of the situation, for I was certain this world is the only one there is. There was nothing for it but to try to become a writer, to invent imaginary worlds into which people might escape at times, as I was able to do when I read a good book. It would be a game. I would fill my time with seeing how far whatever talent I had could occupy my mind before I had to take my place among the shells on the beach, like Mom May, our uncles and aunts Putnam, Aunty Vita and father, for all of them are gone now, and Gene and I have taken their places.

HORNPIPE EPITHALAMIUM

Jack Golab had his jewelry store on West Main Street in Meriden, Connecticut, just a few doors up from the Palace Theater and across the street from the establishment owned by the father of my friend Paul, Wiese's Butter and Egg Shop. Not far above Wiese's there was a record emporium where I bought my LP records, and between them there was, and still is, the silver diner where I learned to love English muffins with bacon and eggs over easy. So this was a hub of my high school life, and that may be why I patronized Golab's Jewelers exclusively.

I gave Jack a fair amount of business. I worked downtown after school and on weekends at Kresge's Five and Dime where I was a busboy making, at first, forty-five cents an hour, and later on ten cents more. With the overtime Kresge's paid me under the table (as a schoolboy I wasn't supposed to work more than — I think it was twenty hours a week), I had enough to carry on a rather heavy dating schedule with the maidens of Meriden High to whom I tended to give, as my token of undying love, an ankle bracelet with her name (and perhaps mine) engraved on it.

But then came the days after high school when I went to sea and left behind my true love, Jean Houdlette, daughter of my seventh-grade shop teacher. When the time came, of course, I had to upgrade somewhat from an ankle bracelet, so I went to Jack Golab's and asked to buy the best ring in the store that a sailor could afford.

The sea blows high and the wind blows cold,
    The *Hornet* sails out to sting.
We bellbottom boys are bully and bold,
Young at the moment but growing old,
And it's no damn good that I bought Jean a ring,
    I bought pretty Jean a ring.

The Gunner's Apprentice is cute as a pin,
    The Yeoman can really swing.
Those almond-eyed girls all know how to sin
To make your eyes swivel and your head spin —
But I had to go buy Jeanie a ring,
    A yellowish diamond ring.

Davy Jones flirts with the mermaids below.
    Down there where Neptune is king
The seacows come swimming along in a row
With nothing more on than a green weed bow
While the drowned sailors gather around in a ring
    And dance till the fathoms ring,

For each wooed a maiden of iron and steel,
    Then took her out for a fling.
She had a pert hull and a lovely keel,
But one day she just wouldn't answer her wheel —
I wonder if Jeanie's still wearing her ring,
    That beautiful bargain ring.

The wind blows cold, the sea blows high;
    I stand here trying to sing,
But the salt spray rises to spit in my eye
Till I'm ready to kill and fit to die
While Jeanie sits home and stares at her ring,
    For I gave sweet Jean my ring.

JEAN

I knew who Jean was three years before she knew who I was. I can actually recall the moment I saw my future wife for the first time. I was standing with a friend — I think it was Jackie Maier — in the driveway of Lincoln Junior High School, in Meriden, Connecticut. It was located near the corner of West Main Street where Windsor Avenue turns into North Third Street. The year was 1946, the month September. Jackie and I had been classmates during the fifth and sixth grades at Benjamin Franklin School farther up West Main, and now we were attending the seventh grade together. If the day were not in fact the first day of the fall term, then it was an early day.

While we stood looking toward the school a pretty girl came out of the side door and walked along the building toward the street. "Who's that?" I asked and pointed.

"Boy, stay away from her! That's old man Houdlette's daughter," Jackie said. I knew who Mr. Houdlette was because I was a member of his shop class. Mr. Houdlette terrified me, as he terrified all the boys, for he was the disciplinarian of the school as well as the woodworking instructor. "I wouldn't want to be her," Jackie went on. "Every night when she gets home he beats her." I made a mental note to stay as far away from Jean Houdlette as possible.

At the beginning of the first woodworking class Mr. Houdlette had called us to order outside the "cage" where most of the portable lethal tools were kept locked up. "It's important that you do exactly as I say," he said in his Down East accent, "because the shop is a dangerous place." He pointed to a bunch of leather straps hanging to the wire grillwork on the inside of the cage. "Do you see those straps?" he asked. "I use those on boys who disobey me. I have to," he said solemnly. He pointed in another direction. "Do you see that machine? That's a band-saw. Let's say you didn't do exactly as I say when you use that machine and you ran your hand through the blade instead of a stick of wood." He paused significantly. "Why, if you hurt yourself, I'd feel all cut up about it . . . and so would you!"

There was a peculiar pause during which conflicting emotions and sensations ran through my nerve cells and my brain. Mr. Houdlette was smiling, sort of. I doubt I knew the word at the time, but it seemed clear to me that he was what I would later understand to be a Sadist. Jackie Maier's description of Mr. Houdlette and the fate of his daughter were credible to me under the circumstances. I felt great pity for Jean, but I was in no position to save her.

That scene in front of the cage sticks in my mind for a reason other than the threat Mr. Houdlette laid on us: it was the first time I was consciously aware of the evil power of a pun. I knew about puns, though, for I had recognized one in a little comic strip that came wrapped around a glob of Double Bubble gum years earlier, when I was in the second grade at Roger Sherman School and my family were living for a year or so on Newton Street on the east side of town. In the first panel a comic character asks another, "How are you feeling today?"

The second figure replies, "I'm feeling pony."

"How's that?"

"A little hoarse."

As soon as I heard Mr. Houdlette's pun and looked around me at the stricken faces of my fellow apprentices, I believe I understood the essential perversity of this form of humor. Though I would always be wary of violent behavior and would go a long way to avoid it, from that moment forward I embraced the pun — indeed, I would often use it thereafter to avoid violence by baffling and confusing an opponent until I could find a way out of the confrontation. It didn't always work, but sometimes it did. It was a good lesson for a future writer to learn, that the tongue can be sharper than the teeth of a band saw.

I lay low in Mr. Houdlette's class from that moment forward — so low, in fact, that in later years he had no recollection at all of me as one of his pupils, though he remembered my younger and much quieter brother Gene who followed in my footsteps through Lincoln five years later. I recall I made a tie rack in shop that semester, with beveled edges and a pine stain.

The next term — my last at Lincoln — I took printing with Jack Conroy, Mr. Houdlette's old friend and his neighbor on Highland Avenue. The two of them and a third teacher, Joseph Nadile, had, before the war, built their three houses side by side, using only each-other's labor. It had been the depression, and local carpenters had picketed them, but I gather they'd done so with little conviction, for the teachers weren't actually hiring anyone to work, after all.

Jack had gone off to the War when it began, and he had only recently returned from Europe where he had served in the Army. All the boys looked up to him as the next thing to a hero, if he weren't one in fact, and nobody feared him, but we all would do anything he asked. He needed no threats. I liked printing better than woodworking, but I can't recall what it was I produced in his class, which was held in the rear of the same shop where woodworking was taught.

The year ended, the summer passed, and I returned to Lincoln the following fall only briefly, for I was to attend Suffield Academy in Suffield, Connecticut, up between Hartford and Springfield, Massachusetts. My father was sending me there, I learned years later, ". . . to save my life," as Gene put it to me in middle age, a notion that astonished me, for I'd been led to believe at the time that Suffield was a great privilege, a financial sacrifice my parents were making in order to give me the best possible boost into the world of adulthood. Besides, though I was pretty mean to him in a standard, big-brotherly kind of way, I never intended to maim Gene permanently. He learned to do quite a good job of that on his own, what with catching poison ivy all over his body after he walked through the smoke of a bonfire; holding firecrackers too long in his hand, and firing a BB pellet that ricocheted off the garage door and split his cornea. It's a miracle he — or either one of us, or any boy, for that matter — survived childhood.

I think the worst thing I ever did to Gene was tie him to the porch when my parents went off somewhere for a while and left me to baby-sit him. I didn't want to be tied down myself, so I made sure he was safe and then hunted up the gang on Windsor Avenue to fool around with. I recall Gene yelled and cried a lot, but as long as I could hear him I knew he was okay.

There's empirical evidence, now that I think of it, to support Gene's claim that I was being shipped away to save wear and tear on the family, for I'm certain my father sent me to spend the first two weeks of the fall term in Lincoln because he couldn't stand to have me around the house while all the rest of the local kids were in school and we were waiting for the term at Suffield to begin in mid-month. He didn't realize it, but sending me to Lincoln was a mistake, for I had nothing to lose there. In the halls I soon met my boon companion Paul Wiese, a hellion greater than I, and together we reduced authority to powder — even Mr. Houdlette's. Miraculously, we got away with it. At least I did.

The two years I spent at Suffield were different from anything I was exposed to prior to the Navy, and the constant supervision produced in me an honor roll student on most occasions. The eighth grade was the third year of Lower School, which was comprised also of the sixth and seventh grades. We boys lived in an old wooden-frame dormitory set off from the Upper School buildings, immediately behind the town library which did double service as the school library. I learned the ropes well enough that first year to decide, at the beginning of freshman year of Upper School, to try my hand at politics. I walked around glad-handing everyone, smiling a lot, being everybody's pal, and got myself elected Class President. It was so easy that I have scorned politics ever since. A politician is nothing but a somewhat classier caliber of used car salesman.

At the end of my freshman year my father's money ran out and I had to return to Meriden to attend high school. One might think I'd have been used to changing schools every year or two, for my family had moved into nearly every quarter of town before the church had purchased a parsonage next door to it, on the corner of Windsor and Springdale, just before my seventh-grade year at Lincoln. I'd spent only one full year in the house, and now I was to leave the boarding-school environment, to which I'd become acclimated if not completely attached; I was once more to be torn from all my friends and classmates to attend a strange school where, without a doubt, I would know no one and would once more have to struggle to make my place. This was not a good example of clear thinking, but it's what I believed.

When I got home I saw an opportunity to make my presence known to the town, my future classmates, and my new teachers before school even began. A local paper, the *Journal,* announced concurrent short-story contests for junior high and high school students during the summer, and I entered. When the results were announced, I had won third prize in the high school category with a piece titled "My Father and I," which I subsequently rewrote many times and eventually cannibalized for another story published years later. The original version appeared in the *Journal* during the summer of 1949, and I felt a little better about people knowing who I was when the fall term began.

At last the much-anticipated and worrisome day arrived. I walked across town, west to east, to Meriden High for the first time with one of my friends from Windsor Avenue, Alle Lamphier, whom I'd known and played with since the seventh grade. He was some comfort.

We climbed the hill to the school, we climbed the long flight of stairs, and we paused halfway up. I looked about with trepidation, but my expression must have changed from worry to amazement and then to joy — for, far from finding myself in an enormous crowd of strangers, I knew everyone! Or so it seemed. Here were all my playmates, classmates, and friends from all the neighborhoods my family had lived in during a period of more than a decade, gathered in one spot.

Paul Wiese from South Meriden was there, in my homeroom with Alle Lamphier, Jack Maier, Curt Offen, Lindsey Churchill (whose father taught English in the high school) and dozens of others from Benjamin Franklin, Roger Sherman, Israel Putnam, and Lincoln Junior High schools; from Lewis, Windsor, and Springdale avenues; Prospect, Curtis, Newton, and North Third streets. There were even people from my Sunday School classes and my church!

My god! It was a convention of cohorts, a panoply of playmates, a midden of merrymakers: Marie Delemarre, whose father ran a candy shop on Liberty Street when I was in the third grade; big Barbara Little, from the fifth grade, still taller than I was; Mary Lou Burke, my girlfriend in the seventh grade (or so I thought of her, since she had been my first "date" — we'd gone to the movies together with a gang of kids), Janice Allaire (the one I'd really wanted to go to the movies with, but she was the private property of Tom Chiovolone, in his opinion), Marie Cantarini from church . . . and Jean Houdlette (who didn't know me, but I knew her).

I no longer had to worry about her father, all I had to do was worry about rejection, for she was both beautiful and quiet. The looks intimidated me, and her silence I interpreted as hauteur rather than the shyness it actually was. With Jean I immediately fell into an adversarial relationship in self-defense, but for the rest of it, I went mad! All the discipline I'd learned at Suffield went out the window. Paul and I immediately resumed the manic behavior we had shared briefly at Lincoln. Among the teachers my short story had some effect, and perhaps it also had an effect among those young people I'd not known elsewhere, but I didn't need its fame, for I was immediately one of the best-known members of the Class of 1952.

Soon I had added to my list of friends all the young men in my homeroom, including Ray Staszewski with whom I was destined to join the Navy in three years, and all the people in the many clubs I joined — the Special Chorus, which broke down into the Men's Glee Club, and then an octet, and ultimately into a foursome, the Sportlanders Barbershop Quartet. Soon a group of us found we were science-fiction readers, and we formed The Fantaseers with its women's auxiliary, The Reesatnafs, of which Jean was a member.

I took to following her down the hill after school as we began the mile-long trek across town to our homes. I dropped jibes upon her rigid back. I kidded her and ribbed her and thought I was being the cleverest fellow in the world — nowadays it would probably be called "sexual harrassment." I suppose I thought this was a way of winning her attention if not her admiration. I never realized that tears were running down the cheeks she kept averted from me, under that crown of light brown, nearly blonde hair — I wonder if I fell in love with her because of the song I'd heard as a child and always felt wistful about, or whether it was her status as the forbidden fruit, or just because I thought she was too good for me and wanted her therefore.

But we never dated in high school. I went out with gaggles of girls. I never did anything beyond heavy petting with any of them, and that is the truth, but my reputation — if only I had known it at the time! — was one of the worst in the school. People assumed that I was running amok among the blushing maidens, but you can't run amok if you date a girl only once or twice. Even my "steady" girls generally lasted no more than a month or two. I spent half my poor pay from Kresge's Five and Ten Cent Store on ID bracelets. Jack Golab in his jewelry shop down by the Palace Theater just loved to see me coming.

When my class graduated and I joined the Navy with my classmate Ray, I broke up with Marge Young, my last high school steady. A year later Jean and I began dating somehow, after a party. I'd come up for a weekend from Brooklyn Naval Shipyard where my carrier, the *Hornet,* was being commissioned, and I'd run into Jean. I cornered her and began talking with her, face to face, I think really for the first time. She didn't move away. She smiled. I dared ask her out.

Not a great while later — about six months, as I recall — I took her to dinner at the Chinese restaurant in Meriden. It was located on the second floor, over some shops across East Main Street from the railroad station. I was still wary of rejection, so I had put some thought into how I was going to phrase my proposal over my favorite meal there, breaded veal cutlets — I don't know why a Chinese restaurant would serve such a dish. It is one of the many small mysteries of a lifetime.

"If I bought you a ring, would you wear it?" I asked.

"Yes," she said.

Afterward, I took Jean home and she told her mother what I'd said. "Oh, Jean" she groaned. "Do you realize what you've done?"

"What?" Jean asked.

"He's asked you to marry him. You're engaged!"

Jean tells me she thought it over and wasn't surprised.

"But what about your college?" Mrs. Houdlette asked — Jean had just finished her freshman year at the University of Connecticut in Storrs.

Her sister Ann said, "Oh, no! He's got the worst reputation in town!" Ann had eloped with a flyer during the War at the age of sixteen and found herself a widow with a baby a year later.

"He's a hellion," her sister Nathalie said with some temper.

Some temper — a good match for that of her sometime Irish-American husband Larry.

"Isn't his father that Italian preacher?" her sister Betty asked. She was married to a chap named "Falton," né "Faltonovich."

I went back to Jack Golab's shop. "What!" he said. "Another I.D. bracelet?"

"It'll be a diamond this time, Jack. Show me what you've got in a wedding set."

Jean and I were engaged two and a half years while I took a world cruise. We were married two weeks before my discharge from the Navy, and a month after Jean's graduation from college in 1956.

During that summer before I, too, entered UConn I worked with Jack Conroy and John Houdlette building two houses for which my father-in-law had contracted, for he had recently retired from teaching. "Lew isn't much on finish work," he told Jean, "but he's all right on framing and rough work."

One might have predicted, I suppose, that Dad Houdlette would turn out to be the kindest man, other than my own father, I have met in my life. Although in his youth he was reputed to have been himself a hellion in school, and in his young manhood he had a hot temper, he had never in her life laid a hand on his youngest daughter, though that claim could not be made in the cases of the elder three.

I remember one scene in particular from that summer. We were building a house in Yalesville, not far from Meriden. Jean's father and I were up on the roof putting down shingles when Jack came along and borrowed our ladder. The sun was out, but it wasn't unpleasant. While we worked, Dad kept up a steady commentary on this, that, and everything in his pleasant Maine accent. He loved to fool around with words, though he was no writer. His favorite author was Joseph C. Lincoln. He used phrases like "garp and swaller" for frothy edibles, and words like "gumshalloobie" for glue or sticky stuff. His preferred curse, when he couldn't stand it anymore, was "Jesus to Jesus and eight hands 'round!"

When we were through on the roof and wanted to get down I called to Jack to bring the ladder back. He grabbed it, hoisted it straight up into the air, and headed for me on the eaves, but he detoured and then began walking in a circle, still carrying his burden. "What the hell are you doing, Jack?" I asked.

"Nothin' much," he said. "I'm just one of the ladder day saints."

"Good grief," I said. "Did you ever hear that 'all cut up' pun of Dad's?"

"Oh, sure," Jack said, setting the ladder against the house. "He used it every term."

"Well, the sun's going down and I'm feeling pony," I told him.

"How's that?"

"A little hoarse."

"Maybe you've caught a colt," he said.

"Jesus to Jesus and eight hands 'round!" said Dad who'd been listening.

"Poor Jean!" say all our friends, shaking their heads. "How long have you had to put up with this?"

"Fifty-two years," she tells them these days. But it isn't all my fault. I had wonderful teachers.

CANCER

When my wife Jean, my son Christopher, five years old, and I arrived in Maine the summer of 1978 (our daughter, Melora, at age nineteen was off living her own life by then), we discovered that my father-in-law John had had prostate cancer for eight years and had not even gone to see a doctor about it. He, his wife Bertha, my sister-in-law Nathalie, and I were gathered in the living room of the old farmhouse when I was told of the situation. Mom Houdlette said something like, "Dad has a growth on his ankle. Would you look at it?" This was an entirely atypical request, for the watchword in the family was go tippy-toe and never ask personal questions.

Of course I acceded. Dad, who was seated, raised his pants leg a few inches. He wasn't wearing socks, only a pair of loafers. When I saw the egg-sized lump I was appalled. I exclaimed — no, I must have shouted — I don't know what I said. I asked questions. The only doctor he had seen was an osteopath in Wiscasset who had told him there was no rush, they could wait until his back was in better shape before he saw a specialist. The problem was that his back was never going to be in better shape, for the prostate cancer that had begun this process of disintegration had metastasized to the spine and then everywhere else. Furious, I wanted them to sue the quack osteopath for malpractice, but of course they wouldn't because they knew, as did I, that it was Dad's fault finally. It was his medical cowardice that had done him in.

So when I had forced Dad to make and keep an appointment with a real medicine man and we were waiting to find out the bad news that wasn't going to be news at all, Jean and I took Mom and Dad to Pemaquid Beach on a lovely summer day. Our daughter Melora has written about this favorite family retreat:

SANDCASTLES

Father carries our yellow pail
Down to where the waves reach,
Dips deep into bluegreen seafoam,
Carries it back sloshing,

(strong black-haired legs all wet),
And empties it into our castle moat.

Mixing just the right combination
Of sand and water, his fingers dribble
Fanciful towers fashioned unbelievably high:
Windows into caverns where fair maidens
Await their heroes' rescues from dragons,
And dungeons are hidden, monsters
Safely imprisoned by salt, sea air,
Bright sun, and clear sky.

But on that last day with the folks before the monsters got out of the castle-keep and came after Dad, though it was the same sort of day Melora described, we knew we were waiting for something indescribable:

We did not know, then, what the wen
  was on his heel. The gulls wheeled
in the summer sun, the combers
    broke and broke; the sand siled.
  On the beach the grandchild ran
  and stopped, dug wells, ran again

while the old man slept in a round
  shadow cast against the light.
The old wife dreamed beside his dream,
    wound in a shawl, as shade
  fretted the edge of waking.
  But all the while, as the tide

pulsed, moving by moments toward
  the drying seaweed of high
water, through the web of his veins
    the crab sidled, stalking.
  The day was perfect, then. Now
  a sea-change has taken it;

rather, it has become two days,
  that fair one and another
in which sandworms rise from the child's wells,

segmented, mandibled.
The beach umbrella sends its shade
casting over the rising surf

to meet the east wind. The seabed
is calm and murderous with
life. The boats toss like dreams, their nets
seining the undertow.
Now the ocean is almost
upon us — our eyes are stars

with spines; our minds are eight-armed; they
grope and coil in the darkness of the sun.

A NEST OF IN-LAWS

Jean, our daughter Melora, nine years old at the time, and I were fine that summer of 1969, but Jean's oldest sister Nathalie, who like everyone else was visiting my parents-in-law at their farm in Dresden, Maine, was setting some of the bats in her belfry at liberty from time to time, and some of them had gotten into the attic. As to the other livestock — we had managed to give away six of the seven kittens, but grandma cat had disappeared, so all that were left were four other cats, three woodchucks under the shed, a family of raccoons who raided the garbage cans every night, a porcupine in the blue spruce, and two toms that hung around waiting for the right moment to replenish the supply of kittens.

I decided to do something about the raccoons. I parked my car so that the headlights would shine on the garbage cans when turned on, and when it got dark I put my nephew Pete, Nathalie's son, into the car and told him to flip the switch on my signal. I hid behind the left fender until I heard a noise, then quietly eased my .22 Mossberg around the grille, and gave Pete the high-sign.

The lights came on and I had the 'coons frozen in my gunsight: a mother and three cubs. I pulled the trigger, but for some reason at the same moment jerked the barrel toward the ground. The animals disappeared at the sound of the shot, of course, but they came back the next night, by which time I had solved the problem permanently. Instead of throwing our scraps away from then on, we just put them on paper plates and let the 'coons eat their supper unmolested on the stoop. They left our cans alone after that.

I caught Melora skinny-dipping at the falls with her red-headed cousin Steve shortly thereafter. I gave her Hell, but before I could catch him he disappeared into the woods and was gone all day. Jean's third sister Anne and her husband Curt, Steve's parents, were worried, but they shouldn't have been, because Fate never allows anything too bad to happen to him. In the evening he returned with a turtle he'd found — I was hoping it would turn out to be a snapper, but of course all the luck was with Steve. The family was so relieved he came back that they wouldn't let me kill him.

My father-in-law John Houdlette and I had started tearing out the old chicken house partitions in the barn, and we'd nearly finished painting the house. The last time, we had run out of paint. Since we did the house in sections over a period of summer seasons, at that moment there were four shades of white on it. Not that painting it did any good anyhow — to save money Jean's dad had thinned the paint of the first coat with so much linseed oil that the house on the river side had turned yellow, though that perhaps had more to do with the pollution of the tidal Kennebec River, of which our Eastern River, also tidal, is a tributary, than the linseed. At the time the Kennebec was so polluted that only anaerobic bacteria could live in it between Augusta and Gardiner, for there was no oxygen at all in the water.

There was a family picnic out in the river yard on the Fourth of July. Uncle Ed, who was almost perfectly round, wanted a ride on the river, so I tied up my aluminum rowboat at the cedar that stuck almost horizontally out over the water, and I helped him down the bank as best I could, but he wound up sitting in the mud with one leg up on the cedar and his head caught in a young hemlock. We managed to get him untangled at last, and he enjoyed the boat ride.

Later on he fell out of the hammock. I heard him talking to himself, but I just turned around and lit my pipe, pretending not to notice. Nothing was broken but his pride. His cocker spaniel Lucky really enjoyed the potato salad.

Aunt Ruth was recently back from the State Hospital. She had committed herself the previous winter, but she declared that she was all right now, though none of us could see a difference. She and Uncle Ray, who loved his beer, had recently celebrated their fortieth anniversary, and we threw a picnic celebration for them. The red-headed cousin broke the hammock, threw one dart up into the elm and another onto the roof, tossed the frisbee into the raspberry patch where it will be found by archaeologists ages hence, stole a box of BB's and shot them out of Melora's pop gun, which I found later after I'd passed over it with the riding mower. He finally left to return to Connecticut with his parents, and things became a *bit* calmer.

Melora kept some of our picnic steamer clams alive in spring water full of table salt and corn meal. Which reminded me that I couldn't get a fish to bite in our muddy Eastern River — I don't suppose they could see the bait — but a five-foot sturgeon jumped and broke water right in front of us as Melora and I came around the bend in the tin boat that summer. There used to be sturgeon in the Kennebec and its tidal tributaries many years earlier, but this was the first one anybody had heard of in a year of blue moons. The Eastern used to be clear water until carp got into it and ate all the plant life off its bed.

Then there was the weekend of the Walk on the Moon. A cousin of Jean's, Joe

Packard and his wife, who also happened to be named Ruth, showed up from Long Island in their hand-built camper. I'd met Joe only once before, and he was a very interesting guy, but accident-prone. They stopped first at Uncle Frank's and Aunt Harriet's house down by the bridge — it used to be the toll house, so that's what it continued to be called. Then they came over to the farmhouse, and I invited Joe to go out mackerel fishing on Sunday morning, before the Moon Landing.

Uncle Frank was Ed's fraternal twin brother, as thin as Ed was fat, and they didn't like each other much. They were nearly eighty, or just over, so I couldn't say no when Frank heard of our expedition and invited himself along.

On Saturday I went into Wiscasset to get some cleats for my fiberglas runabout, which I carted around on a trailer because it's bigger than the tin boat. When I got back home I spent the evening getting together fishing tackle for Joe and Uncle Frank, and early the next morning we headed out for Pemaquid Bay. When we got there the tide was out and we had some difficulty floating the boat. The first thing Joe did was fall while he was shoving the boat off the trailer. He smashed his shin.

We managed to get Joe into the car, and I pulled the boat back up onto the trailer with Uncle Frank getting in the way and threatening to smash himself up, too. I finally hollered at him to get the hell out of the way, which hurt his feelings, but it couldn't be helped. We took off for the nearest hospital, which was in Damariscotta, but by then Uncle Frank had persuaded Joe, who was nearly unconscious because of the pain, that there was better service to be had in Augusta, considerably farther off. I drove there, cursing all the way, and we got Joe x-rays and treatment, finally. As it turned out he had only a hairline fracture, but it was painful enough and put him out of commission. We brought him home, put him to bed, and began nursing him.

On the following Monday Uncle Frank came over with a few mullings — it had occurred to him that he had been trying to go fishing with people for quite a while. The last time he had attempted it, with a lobsterman, his host had fallen and hurt his back. Could it be, he wondered, that he was a jinx? We just kept watching TV — the astronauts planned to leave most of their gear behind. I wondered whether, when we looked at the moon from then on, we'd think of it as an extra-terrestrial land-fill.

Just then old Aunt Ted — my father-in-law's, Ed's, and Frank's eldest sister whose real name was Jessie, but no one called her that for reasons I never understood — phoned and wanted to talk with her nephew, Joe, son of her younger sister Annie (there are lots of duplicate names in my wife's family). He got up on his crutches to go in to the phone, which was in the middle hall.

There's a high threshold where the ell attaches to the main house, and Joe's crutch brought up on it as he was passing through the doorway. We all turned around to see him poised in mid-air, going over backward — it was like a stop-action shot on TV — and then he followed through to land on his back among the splinters of one of his crutches. Everyone's heart missed a beat, but amazingly, he didn't hurt himself again. We picked him up and he decided to go stay at the Toll House with Frank and Harriet. Shaking badly, I drove him over.

That same day, July 21st, was Melora's birthday as well — she shared it with her crippled older cousin Audrey. Owing to all the hubbub and the Moon stuff, which I'd stayed up to watch late into the night, we put off celebrations till the next day, Tuesday. We'd been planning a boat ride at Boothbay for Melora and some of her summer friends, but my undiagnosed lactose intolerance was kicking up so badly I took to bed myself, and Jean and Nathalie took the kids down.

Joe's Ruth couldn't get the camper started to go back to Long Island (she was going to have to drive), and we found out, after we tried jumper cables and what-not, that she'd forgotten to put it into neutral to start it. Joe felt much better after a while. I spent the evening arguing with him, Ruth, Uncle Frank, and Aunt Harriet about Sasquatches, Abominable Snowmen, UFO's, and the Vietnam War (they were all Bomb China hawks). Melora had turned nine; I was thirty-nine going on a hundred and four. I hoped God would spare the yetis, the aliens, the astronauts, and the boys trapped in the jungles of Asia.

Cousin Joe and Ruth stayed for a week, as it turned out, instead of the week-end they'd planned on. The trouble was with the camper, not the leg he banged up. He had built that camper entirely by hand in his basement. He must've had one helluva big door in his basement, but even at that he had to make a folding roof on the vehicle so it would be low enough to get out of the cellar, and whenever anything went wrong with it, it was a federal case to get it fixed. It needed a new bearing in the right front wheel and a new set of mufflers and tailpipes, all of which had to be made to order. The inside of it was amazing.

Joe was an engineer, among other things, and there wasn't one single inch of space in the camper that was wasted. Many years later, in 1979, after the death of Dad Houdlette, he would come back to the farm and we would spend another summer putting his engineering skills to use in turning the ell into an efficiency apartment for Mom Houdlette and Nathalie who were by then living there year-round.

We spent the extra evenings, while he mended, arguing and talking. Two of Joe's pet topics, as I have mentioned, were abominable snowmen and flying saucers — he believed in both strongly. I consider it's just barely possible he knew something the rest of us didn't, he was such an odd bird. To judge from his camper van it could be that the Martians had him working on their space vehicles.

Most of the time he talked about strange footprints and sightings in Upper Michigan, Northern California, and the Himalayas. He wanted to build a boat out of reinforced concrete in our barn. Dad said the boat would make a fine giant set-tub that would look good sitting on one of the mud bars in the middle of the Eastern River. I suggested that when it was finished we crew it with sasquatches and yetis and equip it for interplanetary travel.

Uncle Ed who, when last recorded, was falling out of the hammock, decided to sell his house in Augusta because the shopping district on Western Avenue had grown up around it. His house used to be handy to his pharmacy before he retired. He was quite proud of having been an old-fashioned apothecary. On his front lawn he had placed on display an ancient piece of pharmaceutical paraphernalia. A big sign in front of it said, "DRUG MILL." Uncle Ed was gratified by all the interested young people in blue jeans, long hair, and love beads who stood around on the sidewalk, but he didn't understand why they stared at the house instead of the machine.

Ed kept calling us up and asking us to come out to look at various houses in which he was interested. The first three times we went out we had to prowl around outside because Ed hadn't gotten the keys from the agent so we could get in. The neighbors wondered what we were up to — we could see the curtains moving in their windows. For a while it looked as though Ed and Aunt Sally were going to take a house just outside Wiscasset. It was the first one we'd looked at, and it was advertised at $19,000. Uncle Ed wasn't buying at that price, but once the owners raised the ante to $25,000 he thought he'd take it.

Scalawag the kitten got a tick in his head. Evidently nobody had ever seen a tick in Maine before. We tried to get it out with cigarettes and mineral oil, but neither worked. Finally Dad took matters into his own hands and pulled it out with tweezers. Naturally, he got only the bloated abdomen — the head's still embedded. I keep having weird fantasies about the cat having two skulls, one feline and the other insect.

That weekend Dad and I mowed the field out in back of the barn. I rode the tractor and he followed along behind with a pitchfork to unfoul the cutter bar from time to time. I was going along all right until I looked up to see what Dad was doing. He wasn't there. I looked farther and there he stood, clear across the field. His mouth was moving, but I couldn't hear him over the motor. As I started back in the direction I'd come, to cut another swath, Dad came up rather charily and hollered. I cut the engine to hear him and he yelled, "Bees!" He pointed to the ground ahead of me — sure enough, there they were buzzing up a whirlwind. I'd cut through a nest, and (fortunately) they'd taken out after Dad instead of me.

The incident got him mad, so next day he went out to give it another try and maybe finish the field. The bees were still there, though. He had to let go of the wheel and flail around like a windmill while the tractor went its own way over the ruts. Fortunately, barn swallows looking for an easy meal came up behind him to pick the bees out of the air, and he was finally free of them. I'd gone out to look and one chased me a good distance before it headed back to the hive.

She had been calm for a while, but at last Nathalie blew her lid again. She was supposed to go to Waterville for an appointment with her psychiatrist, but Mom was having a bad time talking her into getting into the car. In my opinion there wasn't anything actually wrong with Nathalie that she hadn't willed upon herself. After her divorce — which she wanted and, in fact, needed desperately, for she and her former husband Larry had fought like the Furies — Nathalie decided her life was over and went into a permanent depression which was relieved only by fits of self-pity and rage because everybody had it in for her and everything was everybody else's fault. To hear her tell it, she and Larry used to live like lovers in the primal Garden.

Instead of getting into the car Nathalie broke loose and came tearing upstairs shouting and swearing like a bo'sun. She slammed the door to her room. I was trying to read in the bedroom across the hall, and I got mad. We started yelling at each other through the wall. I went into her room. She shoved me out and went to slam the door in my face, but I poked my shoe in the door and it swung back. She aimed a couple of roundhouses at me and connected once, so I spun her around, picked her up, and threw her onto her bed.

Just then Mom came up and got between us. Nathalie had somehow gotten hold of the book I'd been reading — I guess it was in my hand — and she sat on the bed fuming and tearing it up. I kept trying to get past Mom to rescue my book, but Mom thought I was trying to reach Nathalie to belt her, which I felt like doing but wouldn't have done, being of the old school. When Mom finally saw what I was after, she stepped aside, I bent to pick up the book (in three pieces), and

Nathalie belted me in the nose. I warned her I'd slap her silly if she didn't cut it out. She started hollering that she was a member of the family too, and had in fact gotten there first, and we were all out to get her. Mom and Dad finally got her into the car and off to Waterville. The next day she didn't come out of her room which was a great relief to all concerned.

Before the summer ended Jean, Melora and I took a trip to The Glen, a hunting and fishing resort on the First Connecticut Lake in New Hampshire owned by my sister-in-law Betty, Jean's second oldest sister. We had fled there to escape the red-headed cousin who returned over the weekend with his brother Jamie and his parents. Some nice weather there, and one day of torrents, but I got out in my runabout a fair amount. Caught no fish, though, as usual.

When we got back we attended an auction at our neighbor's house next door (across several fields). Aunt Ted bought a box full of odd items just to get a particular piece of bric-a-brac, and she gave me the rest of the stuff which included, as it turned out, a real, framed Gibson Girl. I planned to hang it in my office when I got back home — give the place some tone.

Nathalie rescued a gull that had a broken leg and a broken wing: some local kid had shot it with a .22 and left it alongside the road. The folks and Jean and I finally pried it away from Nat who had put it in the shed where it had fouled everything. We took it to Boothbay to give to the wildlife people — they indicated they intended to put it out of its misery. Nathalie nearly had another breakdown. She pointed out to them that the gull was learning to move around very nicely by balancing on its one good wing, its unbroken leg, and its beak. She is very soft-hearted and loves her pets.

Uncle Ed maneuvered Dad and me into a position where we had to borrow Rod Jefford's old pickup truck that had tie-rods so loose it steered like a boat (Rod was a ship's engineer, and he seemed to like the way she handled). We drove it up to Augusta to move some furniture for Uncle Ed. When we'd delivered the stuff, Uncle Ed decided he wanted to ride in the back of the truck, like a kid. He'd had enough after half a mile, and we had to pry him out: he got his foot stuck up on the freeboard of the truck, just as he'd done on the cedar trunk by the river. I've never met a more undignified old man.

On August 27 I got back to the house from the post office where I made out our change of address cards. The summer was about over: The blackberries were huge and ripe, and the milkweed was podding. The hot August weather had broken, and we were tasting fall-in-the-summer while the flowers of our garden were just starting to break into huge blooms. They always did that just as we were about to leave. I'd mow the lawn once more, and then we'd start packing. We planned to leave on Tuesday, the day after Labor Day.

Every year I vowed not to return to Dresden and go through the things the family did, but by May we were always itching to get back to the farm. And now we are retired here. Melora and her family live in the farmhouse, Jean and I live up the road on the same property, and I have a store in the barn. The Mathom Bookshop was established the summer of 1979, after Jean's dad passed away. Her mother followed in 1996, the year I quit teaching, and we took care of Nathalie until she died in the spring of 2002. But there's always a bright side: We get to see our granddaughters, Jessima and Phoebe, just about every day.

VIGILANCE

A father is a night-watch, a patrolman — not every night, perhaps, but fairly often. Probably one got that way early on in parenthood when the babies were small and woke up wailing. And there are always the unusual noises as for instance when the burglar has broken in and your wife asks you in a hissy whisper to go investigate. The burglar has probably managed to abscond by the time you get to the living room; fortunately he has not managed to steal anything.

Then there are the times when, later on, you lie awake listening for your teenage daughter or son (particularly daughter) to get home from a late date.

You stand waiting. You listen.
At your back the house is still,
between the tickings of clocks and timbers.
Beneath the rough soles of your feet
you can feel the cellar stretching to its foundations —
silence in the stone, the furnace brooding.

Shades are partly drawn against
the night. The panes are harder
than ice and as cold. Were you to touch them
they would shatter or seal you in.
The scent of dust is scattered in the air. The breathing
of the stairwell is a deep cascade. Now.

It will happen now: The knob
will turn, the tooth of the lock
take a strain in the cheek of the door where
it is set. You do not ask, "Who
is it?" It makes no mind; it is the wind of autumn,
the winterchase, the sky of change. The hours

flatten on the walls where you
have pinned them; you sense their weight
dragging in their frames against the wire.
A flake of plaster sifts onto

the carpet stretching like a lane of leaves along the
hall. You listen to the respiring rooms

where youth is dreaming age, where
aging sleeps. And you patrol,
you walk the hours listening to nibs scraping,
paper rattling, clocks marking. You
watch the knobs revolve, the windows shake, and in the flue
you hear the cinders rustling to the grate.

THE SHAMBLING MAN

It was at my father's funeral that I first became aware of the figure at the periphery of the crowd, though I suspect he has been around for most of my life. My father died in the fall of 1968 while I was spending the year as visiting professor of English at the State University of New York College at Potsdam. I believe little in prescience despite some of my earlier experiences, and not much more in coincidence, but the Sunday before he died in the middle of that September week I felt a strong urge to phone him. I spoke with him over the phone and asked him to take it easy the coming winter — not to shovel snow in particular. He gave me his word, but I had extracted the wrong promise.

The day of his funeral and interment was a beautiful one, as I recall. The cemetery was large and sylvan. The trees were at the height of their color, and the leaves had only just begun to fall in quantities. The sun was bright enough to sharpen the edges of the breeze, but not to soften its fitful, crisp soughing. With each breath the air launched its vessels of hue upon us as we stood about the open grave. It was a small, deep opening, for my father had asked to be cremated. We had compromised — there had been the embalming and the open casket in the church, but there was only the oblong container here. He had been watching the evening news on television when he gasped, pitched forward, and died. "He wouldn't take his high blood pressure medicine," my mother told me in a whisper while we stood there, her arm in mine, during the brief prayer and commitment. "He said it made him dizzy." We were just about to turn away when I saw a man standing at a distance under an oak, regarding us. I don't know why I took note of him unless it was that he was the only figure within view outside our party. Or perhaps it was something familiar about him that arrested my attention. I believe I thought to myself something like, "Why isn't he standing over here with us?" in a half-unfocussed way, my mind still largely on what my mother had just told me.

The feelings I was experiencing just at that moment were confusing. There was an element of rage in them, a larger dose of frustration, something of despair, but the overall combination amounted to nostalgia and melancholy. The man seemed to sense that I was staring at him; slowly he turned and began to move away. His pace was a forlorn shamble. I couldn't say what he was wearing, but it appeared to be gray. We could hear nothing of his shuffle through the leaves. The memorial moment was over. We turned away before the receding figure was lost among the stones and monuments.

Back at my mother's house I began to say something about my not having been told of dad's refusing to take his medicine, but it was useless — I saw resentment in her eyes, and a bit of the long view down the coming lonely years, so Jean, Melora and I said our goodbyes instead and began our return to upstate New York through the Connecticut hills and western Massachusetts. As we drove I asked my wife Jean whether she had noticed the shabby man at the funeral. "No," she said. "Was he with our party?"

I shrugged. "I don't know. I thought he might be, but maybe not. Maybe he just happened to be there."

"Did you recognize him?"

"In a way. He reminded me of a couple of people."

"Who?" Jean and I glanced at each other. I turned back to the road.

"My grandfather, for one — mom's father. But not exactly." I had been twelve when last I'd seen him twenty-odd years earlier. My mother, younger brother, and I had made a train trip to Wisconsin, the engine and its cars winding through the countryside of post-World War II America into the steam of the engine and the summertime. The windows were open and you got soot in your eye if you stuck your head out.

Grandpa was tall and gaunt. The first thing I did was catch him by his ramshackle barn back of the shanty house, committing an act of nature against the gray clapboards. From then on he left the room when I came in. He imitated smoke. As I entered the room I'd catch a glimpse of him sitting beside the iron stove. He would start, a look like prey in his eyes, and then he'd disappear. I'd heard my mother say, with vast disapproval, that he'd never held a job or read a book in his whole life, but he'd managed to sire nine — six boys and three girls — before time quenched his flame or, more likely, grandma's. It was she who'd held things together.

All the youngsters had grown up inside that shell of boards with floors that waved like the surface of Lake Superior nearby. The seasons had belabored clan and hall, but all had weathered and been weathered, except one sister, Lillian, who had died young. Mother had broken loose and put herself through college, a terrific feat for the times.

But now grandpa had become a ghost who fled from grandchildren, the unruly host sprung from his loins. On that first day he had opened up his fly and soaked the barn. He saw me watching; he turned and faded off. It was my eye, my look of accusation, no doubt, that drove him away. He must have known that, in his daughter's world and therefore in mine, such things didn't occur. I sat at the wheel blushing as I recollected, not his simple act, but my disdain, long since past remedying. There was nothing to do but remember and turn the disdain inward.

By the time we hit the Massachusetts Turnpike and turned westward toward Albany I had conjured another phantom from yesteryear, but its resemblance to the shambling man in the graveyard was as inexact as my grandfather's. I'd been older, a sophomore in high school, and we were leaving the 'forties for the strange and frightening 'fifties. In our English class we'd been studying some of the nineteenth century American poets. When we got to Whitman and "Mannahatta" something in me rebelled. I couldn't have said what at the time, but not long afterward I had gone on a school field trip, it must have been, to New York City for the first time. I remember the bus tour of Chinatown and the Bowery in particular.

It was on the streets of the Bowery that I saw the faded bum that turned me for life against Whitman's willful and insistent optimism. His eyes were the same blue as his jeans, which were, beneath the dirt, the color of sky seen through strata of cirrus. I don't know how I happened to get so close to him, but I could see the thick black soil in the furrows of his skin, the wax in his ears. He had no shoes. His belt was a piece of frayed rope. His threadbare and torn shirt hung out of his pants. He wanted money for wine, and when he got it he went shuffling down the street and disappeared around a corner.

"Watch where you're driving," Jean said. I woke up in time to swerve away from the hitchhiker. "That was close," she said as I steadied up in the right-hand lane.

"Not that close." I glanced in the rear-view mirror, but the hitchhiker was already out of sight.

"Close enough," Jean said, settling back.

"What was that?" Gail asked.

"Sounded like a branch scraping against the window."

"There are no trees near the trailer," she said. "Go take a look, will you?" I got up and started for the door, felt sheepish about my nudity, turned around and pulled on my pants.

Four fourteen years I'd been faithful as a tree. Now I found myself, three years after my father's death, sneaking out to my old friend's young widow to make love in the dead of night, her daughter asleep in the next compartment. The affair had begun as a consolation, but I was not consoled to know that this same sort of thing was happening among many of my compeers — there had already been several divorces, and others were on the way. Trees were falling all about us. The forest was becoming a clearing full of ragged stumps.

The only light in the trailer was a night light, so when I got to the door I eased it open and stuck my head out. I was in time to see a figure sloping away from the trailer, too late to do anything about it. I went back and sat on the edge of Gail's bed. "What was it?" she asked.

I shook my head. "Nothing." I sat for a minute, a sense of humiliation weighing upon my thoughts, which were confused. Then I finished dressing.

"Where are you going?"

"Home," I said.

Not long before my fortieth birthday, which I sincerely believed was going to be my thirty-ninth until Jean corrected me, I had the feeling, the distinct sensation, that someone was shadowing me. I had gone to work in the morning, gone out for lunch, driven home in the late afternoon, feeling jumpy all the while. I had cast awkward glances back over my shoulder, hoping to surprise whoever it was that was dogging me. I thought I had him once. I was on my way back to work at midday when I chanced to glance up and see the reflection of someone in a shop window. I stopped abruptly, creating an eddy in the downtown crowd until I realized that I was looking at myself in the glass, hoping to pick out of the crowd behind me the familiar shape of my tracker. I was unsuccessful.

We had friends over in the evening. One of them, Tom Loe, asked me when my next birthday was to take place. "May 2nd," I said.

"How old will you be, if you don't mind my asking?"

"I mind," I said, "but I'll be thirty-nine." Jean did a take and stared at me. She began to shake her head. I stared back. "What are you shaking your head for?" I asked, annoyed.

"You were born in 1934," she said. This is 1974. Figure it out." I was stunned, but our guests were highly amused. The look on my face must have been a cartoon.

"You and Jack Benny," Tom said. There was nothing for me to do but sink back into the armchair, take another drink, and hate them all.

The summer of 1978, the year Jean's father died, we went to stay with her folks in Maine. We were shocked to see how he had changed during the past year — he had avoided going to the doctor for years, and now it was clearly too late, but we joined forces and made him go at last. While we were waiting over the weekend for the inevitable verdict, we took him one last time to the beach at Pemaquid.

The gulls wheeled in the sun, the combers broke, the sands ran down the beach after the tide. The grandchild ran and stopped, dug wells, ran again while the old man slept in the round shadow cast by the beach umbrella, his wife dreaming beside his dream, wound in a shawl, shade fretting the edge of their waking. At a distance, near the rocks, beyond the sparse crowd of the cool day, I could see a beachcomber walking, his back bent and his eyes on the ground around his shoes. Now and then he would break his uneven gait to bend down and pick something up. Once he half turned and looked back our way. In the clear distance, over the water, Monhegan Island showed itself against the horizon.

The next day my mother-in-law asked me if I wouldn't please dig out the end of the septic tank drainpipe because the tank wasn't draining properly. We had no drainage field, just the pipe dripping into a gully, and mud had plugged it. Jean's father insisted on supervising the job, and he had to stand as close as he could get. "I think you ought to move back a bit, Dad," I told him. "I might slip and hit you on my way down."

"No, no, I'll be fine," he said. But I was digging in blue clay, and the slope of the gully was slippery. I fell, struck his legs, and knocked him down. I got up and stood, horrified, as I watched his face contort with the pain of his cancerous spine. Jean and her mother wore the silence, too, and in the raspberry patch nearby something rustled — a raccoon or a woodchuck, perhaps. "Get me a chair," he managed at last to say, and I slunk away. When I came back I put the kitchen chair beside him — he had managed to get to his hands and knees. Slowly he pulled himself to his feet by holding to the seat of the chair. By Christmas he was dead.

And now I am coming up on my fiftieth birthday. It is a few days away, and I am determined not to replay my fortieth, nor even my thirtieth, when I sat all day in our Euclid, Ohio, apartment with some young friends, students at Oberlin, who had come to visit. I did nothing but complain and act surly. The decades seem to be the hard turns for me. I know others who are bothered by the ones or the fives. But this is going to be the most difficult so far — I have been depressed for weeks. When I look into the mirror in the morning or evening, naked before the glass, I see that slack flesh I used to notice on the arms of my father or father-in-law, the pale skin without tone, the hair going gray, the years doing their duty by my demeanor, but the one inside, staring out, feeling little different than when he'd been twenty-one.

Jean knows what's going on, and she tries to think up breaks in our routine — movies, concerts, pizza suppers. I went out for a pizza the other evening, to a new shop downtown on the corner of Second and Bridge in Oswego. "Pick up one of their menus while you're there," Jean said. We'd heard good reports of their food.

When I came out of the shop with the pizza in my hand I noticed a man, obviously a street person, staggering across Bridge Street toward me, drunk. He made the curb as I was crossing Second toward my car. I put the pizza in the back seat and then remembered the menu. Turning, I recrossed Second Street.

When I came out I looked to my right and stopped. I could not at first comprehend what I was seeing. I might have expected to see it in Whitman's City of Hope and Promise, but not in our town — this ragged man stopped on the walk, his pants down to his kees, his back to me. His underpants were down, too, and he had fouled them — they were loaded with black excrement. He stood there stooped in the drizzle of the empty street, his hand working between his legs, scooping shit out of his pants and throwing it on the pavement.

I looked around for a policeman. I hated that sonofabitch with all my soul and body. I thought for an instant I would walk up to him and kill him. I gagged. Jesus, I thought, why did I have to see this? Why is this happening? I thought of my grandfather and was ashamed, but the shame did nothing to diminish my rage. I thought of the cells rioting in Jean's father's veins, the crabs sidling on the beach, the segmented sandworms' mandibles showing through the moat of the sandcastle, the seabed calm and murderous with life, the boats tossing like dreams, nets seining the undertow.

I thought of the things I'd done to Jean and Gail, of what they'd done to me, what we all do to each other, what we must suffer through merely to die. I looked again at the shambling man now pulling his pants back up. It was he who was the survivor. I crossed the street, got into the car, and drove away home.

THE OBSESSION

In 1979 "Wesli Court" (a pen-name I use for publication of my traditionally formal poems, an anagram of "Lewis Turco") took advantage of the obsessive quality of the sestina's repetitions in "The Obsession," one of the poems in a sequence titled *Letters to the Dead* that rings the changes on the rhymed iambic pentameter sestet. The first line of "The Obsession" contains *all six* of the teleutons (repeated end-words), and the same basic line is repeated incrementally as the first line of succeeding stanzas. Each time the line is repeated the syntax is transposed by hypallage; nonetheless, the line always makes sense. Because all six end-words do appear in this line, a particular problem arises at the envoy, for it cannot be of the required three lines. Instead, the refrain line reappears a seventh time as a one-line envoy rather than as the normal triplet, but with the sense of the original first line reversed:

Last night I dreamed my father died again,
A decade and a year after he dreamed
Of death himself, pitched forward into night.
His world of waking flickered out and died —
An image on a screen. He is the father
Now of fitful dreams that last and last.

I dreamed again my father died at last.
He stood before me in his flesh again.
I greeted him. I said, "How are you, father?"
But he looked frailer than last time I'd dreamed
We were together, older than when he'd died —
I saw upon his face the look of night.

I dreamed my father died again last night.
He stood before a mirror. He looked his last
Into the glass and kissed it. He saw he'd died.
I put my arms about him once again
To help support him as he fell. I dreamed
I held the final heartburst of my father.

I died again last night: I dreamed my father

Kissed himself in glass, kissed me goodnight
In doing so. But what was it I dreamed
In fact? An injury that seems to last
Without abatement, opening again
And yet again in dream? Who was it died

Again last night? I dreamed my father died,
But it was not he — it was not my father,
Only an image flickering again
Upon the screen of dream out of the night.
How long can this cold image of him last?
Whose is it, his or mine? Who dreams he dreamed?

My father died. Again last night I dreamed
I felt his struggling heart still as he died
Beneath my failing hands. And when at last
He weighed me down, then I laid down my father,
Covered him with silence and with night.
I could not bear it should he come again —

I died again last night, my father dreamed.

For a while I thought that this poem had exorcised the dream, but eventually it returned in changed and various forms. I am an old man myself, now, only four years younger than my father was when he died, but still I dream about him, bringing him back to life draped in night shades and the mists of remembrance.

FATHER AND SON

My son, he thinks that I am dead, but it is not true. How can a man be dead if he has sons? He is a good son. I wished that he would be a minister, to follow in the footsteps of his father and to serve God, but it could not be so, and he is a poet instead.

To be a poet is a great honor in my home country, Sicily, so my son honors his father. I wished always to be able to speak the English well, and to write it, but I could not master it. It may be that I can do it better by speaking through my son — I must do it anyway, because my body is ashes, and ashes have not a tongue.

Before I became ashes I wrote a book about my life, and I asked my son to read it and to make the English of it correct. He did not do it at that time. Now he is working on my book — it is a penance; it is his way to put my ashes on his head, as the old monks used to do it. I forgive him, I never blamed him. It is the way of the flesh.

He could not believe in my religion, and it made my heart ache, but as he reads my book, he is discovering that we were closer than he thought. The poet is a religious man too who wishes to know the power that is within and the power that is without. My son believes, but he is afraid to believe, for if he is wrong it will destroy him. This is what he thinks.

I became what men call "dead" on Wednesday, September 18, 1968. On Sunday, the 15th, my son had a premonition, and so he called me from the New York State to Connecticut to ask me not to shovel the snow in the winter. I promised I would not shovel it, but I did not like my medicine for high blood pressure, and so I did not take it. My son cannot forgive himself that he did not find out that I did this, and he does not forgive me.

Now that he has edited my book, my son is writing a memoir for an introduction. I hope it will have not too much sentiment.

The first poem I wrote about my father was titled "An Immigrant Ballad": it appears earlier in this memoir. When it was published in my *First Poems* in 1960 and my mother read it, she took me to task over the poem. How could I say such things, and put them in a book? My father, who had been in the next room and had overheard the argument, came into the kitchen where we were talking and interrupted us. "But it is true!" he said, "It is all true!" The argument must have continued for a while, but that's all of it I remember, because for me it ended with my father's remark, which was typical of him — if a thing were true, it was true, and peace! He believed in the truth, and he tried to live it. No man I ever met tried harder.

I was surprised to discover later, from my cousin, "Little" Josephine, how true the poem in fact was. I had taken what I thought were some poetic liberties — for instance, my father's mandolin playing — but, according to Josie, he had, indeed, played the mandolin in his youth. I had never seen or heard any such thing in our house during the years my brother Gene and I were growing up. Why? Because we were products of his second lifetime, for my father had lived two utterly different lives, one when he was a young hedonist, a second after his spiritual rebirth.

My father speaks, in the first of his writings I have collected in the volume on which I am working, of that rebirth and second life; he refers only obliquely to the first life, as he did prior to his sudden death by heart failure or stroke. What I know of his youth is fragmentary, and it owns the quality of legend. Family talk with my cousins — all of whom are older than I, some of them considerably (two of them deceased early, including one I never met) — who grew up with their uncle as I was to do later, has provided me with some information, but not much. I got even less from my father, who now and then told anecdotes out of the past, but they were few and usually humorous. He lived in the present, and for the future. The past was merely trial, a preliminary to his rebirth, which took place when he was already a man.

One of the stories he sometimes told was of a young man in Sicily who wanted to be Someone, with a capital S. The way to be Someone was to join the Mafia. Somewhere the boy who was to be my sire made contact with a Mafia member who said he could get him into the organization. They made an appointment to meet, and my father went home. Before the appointment he managed to get hold of a pistol. When the time came, he stuck the gun in his belt, feeling like a Big Shot, and set out to meet his contact.

As he was swaggering down the street he heard a commotion ahead of him. He came down to earth in time to notice a cordon of carabinieri coming up the road—they were conducting a house-to-house search for someone. My father, with a very guilty conscience, assumed they were looking for him — somehow they had heard of his appointment to join the Mafia! He jammed the revolver under his shirt, slunk back to his house, and hid, trembling, under the bed.

At last he heard the carabinieri stop outside the door. Through the open window he heard one of them ask, "Whose house is this?" Another answered, "Oh, that's Signor Turco's house. He's a respectable citizen. Leave it alone," and they passed on by.

Under the bed the boy lay, feeling sick and greatly relieved. My grandfather's reputation had saved him — it was, no doubt, a Sign. He got rid of the pistol and never kept the appointment. There were other ways to be Somebody, and he would find one of them. Meanwhile, he would be alive and out of jail.

To hear and watch my father tell this story was to witness a polished comic performance. It was hilarious to see him imitating himself as a Big Shot, the gun stuck in his pants, rolling along the road among the pigs and chickens until the sight of the law froze him in Chaplinesque horror. I wouldn't want anyone to think he was some dour Calvinist or pompous Parson Goodbody.

I understand "Calvinist," but I do not understand "Goodbody." I think it may be too sentimental. I was not a Puritan, but my wife was. She was not an Italian, and that is why, I think, I did not speak so much about my youth in Italy. My wife wanted our two sons to be Americans, and she did not understand my background. She is from Wisconsin, a Methodist missionary who worked with the Italian immigrants. I met her in a camp in Wakefield, Massachusetts, where we both were working with the immigrants, and I was going to be a Protestant minister.

People think it is strange for an Italian to be a minister, but in Sicily is the home of the Waldensians, a very old sect of Protestants, even much older than the Puritans. A Waldensian church is in my native village of Riesi.

But it was not the Waldensians who converted me, it was in this country, the Episcopalians. The men of Sicily are not very religious. It is the women who are religious because they have very hard lives. The men have hard lives, too, but the Roman Catholic Church supports the State, and the State has no interest in Sicily— they think we are all Africans. So the men of Sicily do not support the Church or the State. The Mafia is the government. The Mafia is the only strong power in Sicily.

In this country when I came the Roman Catholic Church was in the control of the Irish people. The Irish people did not want poor people from the south of Italy to be members of their congregations. They did not want other immigrants, either. So, when the Italians wanted to worship, the Irish gave them the church basement to use until they could build their own church, or they gave them nothing.

So it was the Protestant denominations who sent missionaries to help the immigrants, and some of us were converted. But this is a strange thing, too, for there is prejudice everywhere. It is not Christian. Though the Episcopalians converted me, they were not hospitable to Italians, and I had to become a Baptist. Many Italians became Baptists, members of the Italian Baptist Association of America, affiliated with the Northern Baptist Convention. The Italian Baptists had several churches, especially in the East, but in California there also were some.

My wife was prejudiced against Italians too, but I do not think she knew it. She wanted to do good works among them, but she never became one of them. They sensed this. So, in the home I told very little of my old life, and I did not speak the Italian language. My children were raised as Americans. But so were all of the children of the church: the second generation had little understanding of their heritage, and they did not want to know it. Their parents, too, wanted to become Americans, and if they could not do it, then they would be sure the sons and daughters could. Now, I am ashamed that my sons were raised without knowing their father's life and family.

I seem to have been trying to capture my father in words for most of my life, and perhaps he is going to elude me again this time. I remember doing a paper in the eighth or ninth grade while I was enrolled in Suffield Academy, a private, Baptist-affiliated school in Connecticut, where my father insisted I be sent to get the best education possible as he saw it (though my brother Gene tells a different version) and which he could not afford. The paper was titled something like, "My Father: My Ideal." I don't think my father ever realized — perhaps I didn't, either, for a long time — that one important reason I couldn't follow in the path he blazed was that he provided a model for me, and for nearly everyone else who knew him, that most people could not live up to. I saw the difference between what a Christian was supposed to be, and what most in fact were. I early understood the nature of hypocrisy. Rather than be a hypocrite myself, I eschewed conventional piety. I could never hope to be as good as my father, so I wouldn't try.

I suppose my father's life while he was still in Italy must remain mysterious and anecdotal to me, a censored Harlequinade, the juicier parts left out. And I want the juice so that I can conjure him up again in the flesh, for what I don't know about him continues to haunt me. I want him human, not saintly, for I do not understand saintliness and never could, which is why I want to understand him. It is, I think, the central fact of my life that I wanted to be like him and could never understand how he got to be the way he was when I knew him. I could never believe, try as I might, as deeply as he believed, and finally I could not believe at all. The key is buried in his grave, beneath his epitaph:

The good man
is gone. Pray
his eyes see now
what his heart saw.

If there is a note of uncertainty in the words, it is mine, not his.

I loved to read the poetry of my oldest son, and I translated some of it into Italian. I printed some of it even in Protestant journals in Italy, and some is now in a book of Italian-American poetry both in Italy and in America. But my son's poetry was dark, he used dark words, and they broke my heart. God is the light, and I wanted him always to see God. But he is like his mother. The women of her family, the Putnams, are like Sicilian women, and it is strange, for they have a grudge against life. I think that they do not like to be alive.

I cannot tell you what I "see" now that I am ashes, but everything is "light." There are no words. Nothing begins, and nothing ends.

In Italian the name Turco means "Turk," as I wrote in "Deep Ancestry," above. It is not an uncommon name in Sicily. One of my father's anecdotes has to do with the name. During the Turco-Italian War, which took place between the autumns of 1911 and 1912, my father was in the Italian army, stationed well away from the front. One day the officer in charge of his unit assembled the men. He said that volunteers were needed to go to the front lines; those who volunteered were asked to step forward. My father was the only soldier to take two paces and stand at attention. The officer looked him over. "Your name is Turco, no?" he asked.

"Si," my father said.

"What would happen if you were in the trenches? Suppose someone called your name — 'Turco'! The men might think an attack was coming and begin to run. No, no. You step back in line." He pointed to some others of the company — "You, you, you! Step forward!" They had "volunteered," and again my father was spared. Another Sign?

At various points in his youth my father was a miner, a mechanic, a shoemaker, a soldier in the American army — even the chauffeur to the mayor of Rome! I hadn't even known he could drive, for he walked everywhere in Meriden, Connecticut, and never owned a car. He mentions some of these careers in an autobiographical sketch, "A Brief Story of My Life," which I included in the manuscript *The Spiritual Autobiography of Luigi Turco* (see endnote 2 under "The

Story of an Italian Protestant," below). He was also a writer, though his English was never first rate. Still, he had to write at least one sermon a week for many years, some in Italian, some in English. He used to write letters to the local papers in Connecticut, and he wrote articles in Italian and English for *L'Aurora,* the monthly magazine of the Italian Baptist Association of America. The last of these articles, "The Joy of Living," appeared in the same issue with his obituary notice:

LUIGI TURCO
May 28, 1890 – September 18, 1968

The Rev. Luigi Turco, retired pastor of the Italian Baptist Church, now the Grace Baptist Church [of Meriden, Connecticut] died unexpectedly September 18th.

Mr. Turco was pastor of the Italian Baptist Church for 16 years, from 1938 to 1954, later becoming pastor of St. John the Baptist Church, Bronx, N.Y. He returned to Meriden following his retirement 10 years ago.

Born in Sicily May 28, 1890, he studied for a year in the Waldensian Seminary in Rome. He also studied at Rochester and Buffalo Universities and finished his divinity work at Colgate-Rochester School in 1933.

A veteran of World War I, he served in the U. S. Army.

Before coming to Meriden, Mr. Turco served for 12 years as pastor of the Second Italian Baptist Church of Buffalo, N.Y., and as Italian pastor of the Emmanuel Baptist Church in Buffalo for 5 years after founding an Italian mission in that church.

He was ordained into the ministry in April of 1939. Under his pastorate, land at the corner of Windsor and Springdale Avenues adjacent to the original church property was purchased, providing a six-room cottage as a parsonage. Six garages were acquired in the transaction. In addition, a building fund was created from donations by the men of the church.

In 1954, Mr. Turco returned to his hometown of Riesi, Sicily, for a long visit and preached in the local Waldensian Church.

Following his return to the United States in June of 1955 he assumed the pastorate of St. John the Baptist Church in the Bronx, N. Y., where he inaugurated services in Italian for the larger Italian community there.

He is survived by his wife, Mrs. May Putnam Turco; two sons, Lewis P. Turco, visiting professor at the State University, Potsdam, N. Y., and Gene L. Turco of Bristol, Connecticut; a grandson, Steven P. Turco of Bristol; a granddaughter, Melora Turco of Potsdam; a sister, Mrs. Gaetano Mililli, and two brothers, Salvatore Turco and Giuseppe Turco, all of Italy, and several nieces and nephews.

Funeral services were conducted by the Rev. Clinton Barlow at the Grace Baptist Church, 10:00 a.m., Staurday, September [22]. Burial was in Walnut Grove Cemetery, Meriden, Conn. . . .

To Mrs. May P. Turco and her family we pray for the solace and strength that only God can give.

Yes, "The Joy of Living." I enjoyed to be alive, even when life was difficult. My son enjoys to be alive, too, as long as he does not think about it. Many people do not understand him, because he seems to be full of life and good humor, like the men of his mother's family — they were Nordic giants, always smiling. But when he is alone he looks in himself, and the words he takes for his poems paint the darkness of silence and emptiness. So they think his poetry does not fit his personality.

It is the darkness in my son that I am sad about. Still, if he had been a soldier in the trenches, I think he would have volunteered too. To volunteer is to love life so well that there is not the fear of death.

But I have been discouraged. When my congregation in Connecticut forced me to resign because they wanted a younger man, an American, and they wanted to Americanize the name of the Church, I was hurt and bitter. But I would not stop my life. I went to the Bronx in New York and lived in the church bell tower alone. My wife, May, stayed with my younger son, Gene, in Connecticut so he could graduate from the high school there where his friends were. The church in New York was dying, and the people of the Italian neighborhood were moving out. The area was becoming Black. When I tried to do missionary work among the Black people and to bring them into the church, the congregation there became prejudice, and I was forced to leave again. Then the church died.

I came back to Connecticut and began a church in the ballroom of an old hotel. My congregation was my younger son and three old Latvians, refugees that I sponsored after the Second World War against the wishes of my Italian Baptist congregation — they held that against me too. They called me a dictator, but I did not make them do it. When they refused to help the refugees, I took them myself to find them work and a place to live. It was not the church. The Latvian family and my younger son worshipped in the hotel. My wife would not come, and my older son, Lewis, was a sailor in the Navy, far away.

This was my church until fire destroyed the hotel. Again I despaired, but then God told me what to do: write. So I began to write.

Because of my father's near blindness it was extremely difficult for him to read and write, but after his retirement he devoted more and more time to these efforts. Toward the end of his life he became very ambitious in a literary way. The short autobiography was a preliminary to the longer "Letter to My Nephew," who was a Roman Catholic priest in Sicily, which he regarded as his major work and which he tried hard to publish — he even wrote The Beatles to enlist their aid.

On television he had heard something about The Beatles going to India to study with the Maharishi Mahesh Yogi. It reminded him of an episode in Buffalo when he had some sort of spiritual adventure with a yogi. Since both he and The Beatles had shared similar psychic experiences, surely they would be interested in helping to publish his religious book? He never got a reply, so far as I know. Obviously, another crank letter — the incident gave me some insight into crank-hood. "Cranks" like my father, whatever else may be said of them, are true believers, at least twice as real, in all their innocence, as the electric images the rest of us live with in the "real" world. I am convinced that my father was more real than I am, and that is what makes him so ghostly.

It was when I was a shoemaker that I damaged my eye. The husband of my sister Vita left Sicily to come to the United States, and he promised her that when he took a job and saved some money, then he would send for her and his family. So Vita and her children waited. They waited for a long time, but there was no money in his few letters.

So Vita decided to start a shoe factory and to save the money herself. I asked her if I may accompany her and work with her. She said yes, so I worked. One day I was trying to pull a nail out of a shoe with pliers. The nail came out suddenly and it went into my good eye, so I was blind in that eye. The other eye was not good.

But we saved the money, and we took a ship. When we came to Massachusetts we found her husband working in a tavern and drinking. We lived in squalor. The baby was in an orange box, and a rat crawled on her. I began to tell my sister that I would save the family, that her husband would not do it, that he was not a good Christian. And so I began to study. I finished the high school, and I began to study for the ministry.

But look at the dark words of my son in his poem. I do not understand it, what he says, but it does not sound correct. The "wings" do not "fail me." The "wind" does not "blow from darkness into dark." I have no "tricks to sustain me." It is my son speaking not of me, but of himself, as he did on the epitaph that he put on my stone.

He is full of doubt.

My father's story had come to haunt me by the time he was living in the house he and my mother had bought on South Avenue after years of moving from one neighborhood to another. But the house in which I remember him best was the parsonage. We moved into it when I was in junior high school, before I went to Suffield. After years of planning and saving, the church had bought it, and for a while we had some feeling of physical location, a point of reference, and a neighborhood.

The parsonage was my great pride. For years the church saved to buy it. But it was only one house that we lived in, and my son does not remember much the house in Buffalo where I lived with the family of my sister Vita. I was the head of that house too. We went from Massachusetts when I became a minister, leaving the husband behind. I converted my sister and her children and took them out of the squalid surroundings. My nieces, when they grew up, did not like it that I took them away from their father, but my nephews who were older remembered what our life was like, and they continued to honor their uncle.

When I was married, my nieces called my wife "The Great Dane," because she was half Danish, but she loved them and was good to them. None of them approved of my marriage, not even my sister Vita. But my wife and I were almost too old to be married, thirty-four and forty-four years, and we wanted a family of our own. Ah, the things that people will do in the world! It was not a happy marriage, but we raised our two sons, and they are good sons. We have done our duty.

After he had written his autobiography and his "Letter," at the very end of his time, my father worked largely on translating some of my poems into Italian — not out of any literary consideration, but out of a desire to understand his offspring. This is clear from some of his letters. He thought in Italian, and in order to communicate he had first to translate his thoughts into English. The reverse was true as well — in order to understand English, he had to translate into Italian.

Perhaps that's all there is to it: the language barrier — I speak no Italian at all, though I took high school Latin and college French and can read it a bit if I have a vocabulary handy. I have always regretted that my father did not teach me to speak his language, but the byword in those days was "assimilation." Perhaps our groping to understand each other is merely a matter of words. At any rate, that is all we have now. On September 16, 1957, he wrote me the following letter. I will leave it as he wrote it, as an example of his pure style:

> Dear Lewis,
>
> Next month I will start a church in one of the rooms of Winthrop Hotel. Dr. Ervin Seale, pastor of the Church of the Truth of New York City, will come to Meriden to help me starting the church.
>
> I had a letter from Dr. Uheler, a psychologist and cooworker with Dr. Seale, telling me to write a long letter to Dr. Seale in which he could see the progress of my ideas concerning the movement of The New Thought on which Religious Science Churches are based. Instead of a long letter I wrote to Dr. Seale a brief story of my life which, the enclosed in this letter, is a copy. There he will see far better than in a letter how I came to the knowledge of the New Thought movement, which is not new at all; It is as old as Christianity is, but the teachings of the Bible have been obscured by the numerous dogmas and creeds which churches, both Protestant and Catholic, have been formulated through the centuries.
>
> I am sending this copy to you of the story of my life for correction of my English. My greatest trouble is my English Language. I am determined to master it as best as I can. So, please teach me as much English as you can. Correct this paper for me and when you come to Meriden show me all my mistakes of grammar, punctuation, construction, ect.
>
> Next Friday I shall go to New York and have an enterview with Dr. Seale to discus plans for the starting of the church. I shall be back late in the evening, (Sunday)
>
> Enclosed you find also a card of congratulation from the Meriden Saving Bank which I opened thinking that it was my mail. This lead me to congratulate you, too. How? By a gift of $25.00. Let me buy the text books for you this year, so you owe me no money.
>
> God bless you together with your sweet wife,
>
> Your loving father. . . .

It is even more difficult to speak now, using the voice of my son. But he has come to believe some of the things that I believed at the end of my life. Still, there is the darkness that comes to him sometimes, the darkness that he sees instead of the light.

I do not think that I will speak again, but I will remain with him. Nothing is finished. Forever we are with one another, the all of us, living and the dead, the born and the unborn.

MINOTAUR

Because I am a "formalist" (in the broadest sense of the word, meaning, "one who is interested in the manifold ways in which poems may be written"), readers also often assume that I am exclusively a *rationalist,* one who writes with his conscious mind. But "Minotaur" is a poem that grew directly out of a clearly recollected dream. Whenever I dream a poem into existence, I try to approach the subject directly, putting on paper as clearly as possible exactly what I can recall of the experience. Nothing fancy, merely crystalline narrative, for if the dream is to work for others as it worked for me, it must be experienced, at least vicariously.

In my dream there is light
in the underground passage
turning between stone block walls.
The floor is a shallow stream.

How have I come to be
here in this place with my son,
not yet a yearling? Danger
waits nearby — one can feel it.

He must be preserved. At
the end of the passage there
is safety — another thing
I know, but cannot tell how.

The water moves slowly,
but it can bear him in this
frail shell in which I place him.
And he has been set afloat.

As he drifts through stone, through
light, he rises, leans upon
the rim to fathom water.
It is true: Pain is depthless.

My feet move to follow,

to seat my child again, but
the fluid drags at my flesh.
I call; he does not look back.

As he diminishes
in the curve of his passage,
I sense the beast I have feared
in the distance between us.

However, during the dream I did not think of Minotaur, the bull-headed man-monster that inhabited the Cretan labyrinth and devoured the youthful subjects of King Minos. This image was a conscious, waking one, albeit straight out of Jung's pantheon of archetypes: the inhabitants of the unconscious psyche. In my dream I knew there was a menace lying in wait in the tunnel — I thought I stood between it and my little son whom I set my adrift in order to save him. But I was wrong, for the monster stood now between us, between my son and me. What was the nature of the monster? Was it time, or growing up, or simply fate? Perhaps none of these things, perhaps all of them.

Once the poem was finished I did need a title, though. At the time I was writing and juggling poems for a series of poems, an alphabestiary of imaginary creatures to be titled *A Book of Beasts.* Some of these, the humanoid monsters, were published in a chapbook titled *A Cage of Creatures* in 1978. I must have needed a poem to represent the letter **M**, and perhaps that is what caused me to think of "Minotaur" as a title for this piece which was later published in another chapbook containing most of the rest of *A Book of Beasts: A Maze of Monsters* (1986 — *A Book of Beasts* has never been published as a unit to this day).* At any rate, clearly, formality and rationalism had very little to do with this poem, but dream, and serendipity in the form of an ancient myth, had everything to do with it. But there are terms even for the unrational things I did, and the central image of this poem is what T. S. Eliot called an "objective correlative," an "object" (the Minotaur) that corresponded to the idea I was trying to get across.

*This is no longer true; see my collection titled *Fearful Pleasures.*

THE GLASS CUP

When I fought free of the dream I saw it was light, but early. I closed my eyes again — the dream lurked there still, beneath my lids, behind the eyes.

(I saw the infant lying on the bed in Doctor Dentons, obviously deformed, but the precise nature of the misshaping obscured by the pajamas.)

I struck full awake finally. I pushed the button of my digital watch and saw it was a minute or two after six in the morning. I sat up on the day-bed, for I had spent the night in my air-conditioned garret study rather than in the bedroom on the second floor. The early August weather was sultry.

I tried not to make a lot of noise as I got my breakfast, but Chris, my five-year-old, smelled the bacon frying and came down. He had already dressed. "Good morning," he said.

"Good morning, little pal. Want some bacon?"

Chris nodded. When he'd had his breakfast he went out to ride the hazy morning sidewalk on his Huffy bicycle — he spent most of every day on his bike. I had seldom seen a child so young so expert on a two-wheeler. I loved to watch Chris ride, a tall boy with tawny blonde hair, the color his mother's hair had been when she was young. Chris looked like Jean — "Thank God," I always said when my friends remarked upon it, and people laughed.

(Jean had been in the dream too. We had arrived dressed for a formal visit at the run-down house — or was it a slum apartment? The setting had been urban. We had been invited by the man — I could not imagine knowing such a man well enough to be invited to his home: thin, dirty, silent, with large washed-out eyes, hungry eyes, something mean about them, mean and cynical, but fearful as well.)

What could it mean, if anything? I had never been inside a house like that in my life, though I had gotten a glimpse into one just a few days before, in Richmond, Maine, when we had still been on summer vacation. Chris and I had gone over together in grandpa's pickup truck to get some fishing gear for Chris, and we'd run into Richmond Days and a parade — high school band, lots of fire engines from all over Lincoln County. That had been a hot day too, at the end of July.

As Chris and I had walked up the hill toward Ring's Hardware we had passed a house that seemed to be falling in on itself, the porch collapsing, the siding moldering. The door had been standing ajar, and I had glanced in. There had been an ancient sofa visible, piled with broken toys, dirty clothes. It sat in the middle of a trash heap. I had actually been embarrassed, had flushed and looked away quickly, as though I had inadvertently caught the inhabitants in an act of incest. I'd glanced to see if Chris had noticed anything and was relieved to see him staring at the parade.

"What are you doing up so early?" I looked up from my coffee. Jean poured herself a cup and sat down.

"Bad dream. Couldn't get back to sleep."

"Oh. I thought once we got back you'd be able to start getting some rest." She sipped — she liked hers black. I always added three teaspoons of honey to my favorite mug, a round cup made of thick glass with a map of the world painted on it. Our teen-aged daughter Melora, whenever she saw me loading up, accused me of drinking syrup. I liked to hold the cup in both hands while I drank, even though it had a handle. I enjoyed the conceit, banal as it was, that I held the world in my hands, controlled it, and took nourishment from it as well.

"What was the dream about?" Jean asked.

I shook my head. "I don't want to talk about it, it's still with me. You were in it." Jean raised her eyebrow. I shook my head again. "You were in danger," I said.

(We had gone in, and the man had taken my coat. Why had I been wearing that coat? — light over-jacket, really. Where had I gotten it? Some down-at-the-heels place years ago, a "bargain": yellow, fuzzy. It had immediately lost its shape. Jean had hated it, but I'd worn it a lot until she had expropriated it, thrown it away or given it to the Salvation Army. The man had disappeared with it. Jean and I had seated ourselves on the sofa.)

"Is Chris out?"

I nodded and got up. "He's eaten. I'm going up to my room. I have to start getting ready for school to begin."

Jean looked at me. "Already? It's only the beginning of August. The College doesn't start until after Labor Day."

I started down the hall. "I have that writing project to finish up. That's why we came back early, remember?" I said over my shoulder.

"Is that the reason?" she called as I started up the stairs, but I didn't answer.

I spent an hour or so typing until I heard Chris on the attic stairs. I was relieved when Chris said, "I want to go to the playground."

"Sure, pal," I said. We went down and got our bikes — this was a morning ritual. We pedaled down the block of middle-class homes under the maple and horse-chestnut trees, which I loved. For some reason this section of upstate New York had not been riven of the chestnuts — they were tall and healthy. My mother-in-law had wanted a seedling for the Maine farm, and I had brought one up to her in July. She had been delighted.

We coasted down the next block, a steep hill between the grassy Sylvan Glen apartments on the left and the great old Victorian mansion, also now converted to apartments, across the street on the right. Some of my academic colleagues lived in both places.

At the bottom of the hill was Breitbeck Park and the playground, directly on the shore of Lake Ontario. It was a new park — the trees needed twenty years more to make significant shade, but it was a pleasant place nevertheless, with winding walks Chris and I could ride over and over until we got tired and sat on a bench to talk.

"What's wrong with Grandpa?" Chris asked, nestling under my right arm. "He's in a hospital."

I didn't answer right away. I thought, instead, of the ripe tumor on my father-in-law's heel when we arrived, the old man afraid to go to a doctor, and the family afraid to force the issue — so I had done it. The biopsy. The confirmation, the tests to find it had spread everywhere.

But there was no way Jean could claim I'd fled from that situation specifically — the two old people and the divorced and unstable eldest sister in the house alone, now that the hospital had sent Grandpa home to die. "No, he's not in the hospital now. He's back home at the farm. He went back after we left."

"Is he all right now?"

"He's still very sick," I said.

"Is he going to die?"

"Everybody has to die."

"I know it," Chris said. "We go to the cemetery to see them in Maine."

I nodded. It was the morning ritual in Dresden — the cemetery just up the road at the bend, filled with Jean's relatives. Those who were still living were nearly all old, and every summer for the past several years one or two of them had been ill or had died. One, her cousin Richard, had actually been a year younger than Jean and me. There were more summers to go.

Last summer I had sent Jean and the children up alone while I spent six weeks writing at Yaddo, an artists' colony in Saratoga Springs. This summer I couldn't avoid the trip, but I had been awarded a fellowship to finish a book. Before we'd gone to Maine I had made it clear we couldn't spend both months on the farm — for the first time I'd taken none of my work along, and it had been good planning, though I couldn't have known that this time it would be Jean's father.

Before the diagnosis had been confirmed the doctor had taken me aside and told me he was sure it was cancer. Jean wouldn't let him tell her mother — "Let her have another week" — so I had lain those seven nights, all night, thinking about my father-in-law.

Whenever I would be drifting off to sleep the tumor would blossom in my mind, and I would be startled awake again to toss in the hot night until dawn, or get up and go downstairs to read.

I looked at Chris now and felt apprehension and guilt again, but I could not tell why. Was it because one day I would put my son through this? It had been easier when my own father had died though, again, the doctor had warned me five years earlier it could happen at any time, suddenly, which is how it had taken place: a pitching forward while watching the news on television, a rattle, and that was all.

Even at that, I had dreamed. I had dreamt until I had written it out in a poem, and that had exorcised my father so that only mourning remained to flower at odd moments, often in the garret where his picture as a young man looked down at me from the wall above my desk.

This new dream, however, seemed to be different. It seemed to have nothing to do with Grandpa, though it had relationships with Maine. The infant on the bed, for instance: I groped for associations, for similar feelings, and the only image I could produce was the dead animal — squirrel, perhaps — I had found in the well one year.

When the old well on the hill across the road had run dry, Grandpa and I had dug out a spring of the purest water in the old pasture, put in concrete tiles, and piped the liquid a hundred yards to the house. Three summers ago, when Chris had been two, I had gone to check the wellspring. I had found that someone had somehow pushed the heavy concrete cover aside and a small animal had fallen in — it was decomposing and lying on what seemed to be a bed of straw that vandals had dropped into the tiles.

I had gone back to the house to report what I'd found and to tell the family not to use the water. I'd gotten some Clorox to pour in as a disinfectant, and I took along a curved, three-tined garden fork with which I fished out the animal. It was the animal that the child in my dream reminded me of. I had tried to pull out the straw as well, but I found that it was in fact a bed of roots, the roots of the small trees that had grown up around the wellspring, forcing their way through the seams of the tiles. I'd gotten as many as I could and replaced the cover, then cut down the closest trees. This summer I had checked again, but no one else had tampered with the spring.

That day Chris had gone with me. We had followed the pipeline down along the high riverbank, at the foot of the meadow back of the barn, and checked on the pump house, too. Once, snakes had gotten in there — one had somehow got caught in the works, and the pump had needed to be rebuilt. But the system this time was all right.

Chris and I had gone on through the young copse surrounding the spring, over the old blueberry field, toward the cemetery. I had had to carry my son through the high grass, nearly till we'd reached the dirt road leading to the graveyard. From there Chris had led the way. He'd made straight for the newest of the Houdlette plots.

"Is this my cousins?" he asked.

"Your cousin, and your aunt, and your great grandma and great grandpa." The day was very warm, but the large trees, some of them still elms, cast good shade, and we rested.

"I remember my cousin. He gave me a ride in the wagon." I marveled, again, at Chris's memory — cousin Robert Houdlette, Aunt Ted's son, two summers earlier had given him rides in a lawn wagon attached to his riding mower. "Was my aunt old?"

"Aunt Jessie was really your great-aunt, and she was very old. She was ninety-six. She was Grandpa's oldest sister."

As we started back Chris climbed on a stranger's headstone, and I had to explain that people might not like his doing that. The headstone wobbled, too; it looked as though it might break.

When we had gotten back to the farm I had returned to the book I had been reading — Kurt Seligman's *Magic, Supernaturalism, and Religion.* Perhaps that was where I had found the prototype of the woman in my dream, now that I thought of it. I would have to check it out when Chris and I got back from the park.

(When the man in the dream had returned to the living room he had introduced Jean and me to his wife. She was a stocky woman, very lively — too lively. The man had receded into a corner while she carried on a monologue. I remembered no words in specific, but the tenor of the one-sided conversation became very suggestive. The woman primped and gyrated before me — excepting for a glance now and then, she ignored Jean. Jean and I began to grow uneasy, exchanging apprehensive and startled looks. The man began to — "smirk" wasn't quite the right word, his eyes going back and forth between his wife and his guests. Then she had taken off her blouse under which she wore nothing. She began flaunting herself, offering herself to me. She had four breasts. I experienced a sense of revulsion, panic, and imminent violence.)

"Dad," Chris said, "let's go home."

"Right, pal." we got on our bikes and pedaled up the hill. Chris was very strong — I admired the sturdy legs as they worked, seemingly without effort, on his gearless bike. By the time we reached the top of the hill I was tired, though I had five gears and had gone up in low. When we got home Chris went to play with Tim, the boy next door.

I went up to my garret to find the Seligman book, which I'd never finished, but I could find no reference to a four-breasted goddess in the pages I had read. The closest I could come was a picture of the god Moloch, with seven apertures in its chest. I put the book aside and thought again about the dream. Immediately all the strange emotions came back.

(All I could think of was how to get out of there. I told the man and his wife — suddenly I remembered the fifth person in the room, a shadowy figure, a woman in a wheelchair — that Jean and I really had to be going. Might I have my shabby yellow coat? The man went to find it, and time lengthened unbearably. When the man returned he said he couldn't locate it. Was I sure I had one when I came in?

For the first time in the dream situation I felt a surge of anger, but my desire to get Jean out of danger prevailed. I said, Well, never mind, I'd pick it up some other time. I took Jean by the elbow, led her to the door, and we went out. It was cold.

In front of the house anger welled up again, very strongly. "Go to the car, get in, and lock it," I said to Jean. "Wait for me. I'm going to get my coat."

Her eyes were wide and fearful as she replied, "Don't go back in there."

I pushed her away and waited till I saw her disappear into the darkness, for it was night — had it been night when we arrived? I went back and knocked loudly on the door. The man opened it, and I pushed my way in. "I need my jacket," I said. "It's chilly outdoors."

I brushed past the man and went into a bedroom. When I looked down, the child was asleep on the bed in its Doctor Dentons. I could not identify the feeling that centered itself in my throat. The baby lay there formless and silent. I searched the house but could not find the jacket. The man sloped behind me through the rooms, as did the woman — an older woman, but not an old one — in the wheelchair. I could feel almost physically the malevolence and hatred at my back.)

When the phone rang I knew it was Jean calling me downstairs for lunch — we had learned from some students at the college how to use the phone as an intercom. At the table we ate in silence, even Chris who was in a hurry to get back outside. Over coffee Jean said, "I'd like to call the folks."

"Go ahead. I'll go upstairs and get on the extension." I watched her dial, and by the time I lifted the receiver up in my room Jean was talking to her eldest sister, Nathalie. After five minutes of my sister-in-law's aimless chitter-chatter I silently hung up, furious. I had very nearly told her we had not called to listen to her ask questions they had discussed only a few days before in Maine. I lit a pipe and smoked.

Nathalie was a child created with over-kindness from a failed adult. Long after her divorce she had been plucked out of her sordid home and taken by her parents into their Maine retirement. There were still tantrums, introversions in which everyone but herself was held to blame for her spoiled life. I remembered the funeral of Uncle Alfred three years earlier, at which I had, once again, served as pallbearer. Nathalie, at the last moment before going to the funeral parlor, had wandered off into the fields, tearing off her clothes and scattering the rags among the milkweed and raspberry bushes. My father-in-law had sent them all on ahead while he tried to cope with his first daughter.

At the funeral there had been a handful of people, mostly relatives from nearby. Alfred's wife, Aunt Mabel, sat weeping in the front row with her crippled daughter Audrey who was in her wheelchair. A victim of childhood measles, Audrey had been only barely ambulatory for years — unnecessarily so, was the rumor of the family. "She could do more if she wanted to," Aunt Ruth had said more than once.

The measles had led to encephalitis, and that to a life of bitter spinsterhood. Audrey had always reminded me of Nathalie, even when my sister-in-law had been married and a teacher. Now, suddenly, she also reminded me of my dream, of the woman in the wheelchair.

When I judged Nathalie had spent herself talking with Jean, I picked up the phone again — she was still on the wire, but from the conversation and Jean's lengthening silences I could tell she would turn the instrument over to her mother shortly. I waited until she did so.

There was no change, of course. Jean's mother sounded sad and tired, and her father was almost inaudible when he spoke. When everyone had hung up, I went back downstairs.

"Nathalie is acting pretty well," Jean said. "She's responding to the situation better than I thought she would." She sighed. "Still, I feel guilty about not being there." Neither of us mentioned what we both knew — that I was angry about Nathalie's wasting all that phone time.

"You have two other sisters besides Nathalie," I said. "Betty is a widow, and Ann has three grown children. They both live much closer to Dresden than we do. You have a five-year-old son about to enter school. Why can't Ann go back up for a while? Is she afraid her husband will starve to death?" I finished my mug of coffee and made a face — even with the honey in it, it tasted bitter, metallic. I put it on the table and pushed it away.

Jean brooded into a second cup of coffee. "Betty has her resort to run, and Curt can't cook."

I snorted derisively. "Anybody can cook. You mean won't cook. Ann left two of her kids alone at home to go up to Maine for a couple of weeks last month, and they managed to fry hamburgers while she was gone. I guess Curt could do the same. Or the kids could cook for him." I knocked my pipe out in an ashtray. I knew subliminally that my anger was only guilt transformed and my arguments were — though logical and reasonable — only rationalizations. With an effort of will, I suppressed the thought.

Jean got up to wash the dishes. I went out and sat on the front porch. I watched Chris and Tim, the neighbor boy, racing and doing wheelies on their cycles on the summer sidewalk. They were both very good, though naturally Tim, who was older, was better than Chris.

(I could stay no longer. I pushed the man aside and went out of the house again. The man followed me, muttering, saying insulting things under his breath; then, once they were outdoors, he got louder.

I turned to look at him. He was crouching in the dirt, his eyes bloodshot moons. He picked up a glass cup that was lying on the ground and, from his awkward position, threw it at me. It shattered at my feet.

I snarled, a string of disgust and loathing running down my throat, though whether for myself and the way I felt about the man and his family, or for the man himself, I could not have said. I bent over and picked up a sharp shard of the broken glass. I looked at it and saw that part of the northern hemisphere of the world was painted on it. I raised my arm and hurled it at the man.

The glass sailed true, struck him on the forehead. A gash opened and blood began to run down over the man's brow and face. I turned and went to the car. I slid in beside Jean and, in slow motion, we drove away.)

Just as we had done the week before.

CONCEIT

Doctors call it having a "sleeping disorder" when one has insomnia, but in fact it is always night when the brain is most active, whether asleep or awake. Even if one isn't a writer poring over words on a piece of paper, inventing fables, trapping myths, shooting griffons and unicorns with a sharp pen, one's brain is doing the same thing though we don't remember what it is we have dreamed. I think that a large part of the difference between a writer and one who does other things is that the writer somehow remembers at least scraps of what he or she dreams. On the other hand, however, perhaps

If I were you, I wouldn't listen
to me. If I stood there in your shoes,
staring at this graying man writing
in an attic late at night, a motor snoring
and music trickling from speakers
to seep through a sleeping house,

I would turn away, thinking of dreams
I have had, wondering if I'd have more
someday, some night, some winter morning,
the blue of the lake dripping out of its ice, wind
sniffing at the window. But spring
will have come by then. If you

were I you would be grateful. You'd say,
"Listen to that nib scratching, the grass
struggling up through drifts of sleep, these words
forming themselves as though they meant something to me."
You would say, "Over the chimney
of this house night is lifting

beneath the wings of geese returning
to their old haunts." And I would reply,
"They have never been away. All is
as it was, as it will always be." Then, shaking
your head, you would turn your back, you

would leave me here just as I

would leave you, if I were you walking
down the stairs, yellow light cascading
out of the ceiling, along the eaves,
into the rooms full of sleeping people whose love
will wash through our dreams of waking
when we shall lie down at last.

THE WATCHER

I have felt now and then — more frequently as the years passed — as though I were an actor in some cosmic play for which there is no audience. I am prone to feeling that way when I least expect it, as for instance when I am playing with my cat Seeger — a lean, all-black, half-Siamese feline with an attitude who had been named by my son's rock band.

Seeger loves to wrestle. When the cat is being an absolute pain in the ass, rocketing around the house in a madcap race to nowhere, sharpening his claws on the furniture, or bedeviling Sally, the sixteen-year old tabby, I will put on one of my leather work gloves, get down on my knees on the living room carpet, and challenge him.

Seeger is fast, but I am usually faster, though I have a lower armful of thin white scars to show that I am not always so. As soon as we begin to fight Seeger begins to purr, of all things. It makes me grin. And then, because without warning sometimes I feel eyes lying upon me, I will cast a glance behind me, over my shoulder, to see who is watching. My hand will freeze in the grip of the cat on its back, my fingers working his belly, Seeger raking the palm of the glove with his hind claws. Never is anyone there.

Nor had there been since I was twelve years old. That was when I had lost my religion — if in fact I had ever had it, but I hadn't told my preacher father for several years more. Up to that point I had felt as though God were keeping an eye on me, judging me, marking off points on a tally. Finally, when my father had said one too many times, in one way or another, that I was expected to follow in the paternal footsteps and accept the priestly vocation, I had said, "Dad, I don't want to hurt you, but I'm not going to do it."

"Do what?" had been the innocent question, or had it been so innocent? Why had the old fellow (old enough, in fact, to be my grandfather rather than my father) brought up the subject so often? Wasn't it because he had known all along, or at least suspected, that I had had no calling?

"Become a minister," I had replied.

"What!" My father's deeply lined face had taken on a stricken look. "Why not?"

"Oh, you never loved us," mother had said from the doorway where she had been eavesdropping.

That had made me angry. Mother had always had a way of doing or saying exactly the thing that would infuriate her older son. "Of course I do!" I had said. "But the Lord never spoke to me. I listened, but I never heard a word," I said. "I can't believe in all that stuff."

No voice had ever spoken to my father, either, I am quite certain. From the things he had said I had gathered that it was the one great anguish of his life. He had wanted to experience revelation, to see a vision, but it had never happened. However, it had evidently happened to my mother, once, when she was a Wisconsin farm girl, and from that moment she had been determined to become a missionary. She had succeeded, but being a mother and the wife of a minister, especially an Italian minister, had eventually put her vocation into second, perhaps even third, place in her life.

I can remember none of the enormous argument that followed my denial of my parents' religion, or religions, as the case might be, for no two people's beliefs are ever identical, which is no doubt why the churches are always catechizing their adherents, and why those adherents are always splitting off into new sects. After that day the subject had seldom been broached, though I was still expected to attend church and take part in the activities of the parish.

I left home to join the Navy when I was eighteen years of age. I had never gone back to live, only to visit briefly over the years. Through the years I would now and again experience those cosmic eyes on my back, glances left over from all that indoctrination, no doubt.

Certainly, no one ever was there when I looked. The only observer was I. Sometimes I would see myself step back and look at what I was doing, as though I were a spectator in a scene I had written. Even when I had heard the voice in boot camp I knew it must have been my own and no one else's, for it had come from inside my head, though it had seemed to be disembodied.

I had been walking on a tarmac in Maryland in broad daylight, on a day in 1952, yet I'd had the physical sensation of walking at the center of a pit that traveled with me. I could not see over the edge: four interminable years of enlistment stretched before me. The sun in the sky could not penetrate the darkness that engulfed me. My loneliness had been absolute. There was only one way out that I could see, and that was to take my own life.

But at that moment I had heard, clearly as a clarion, a voice in my head that said, "Wait and this will pass." I had known the voice was right. I didn't feel it was true, I knew it was. I had taken the advice — my own advice, without a doubt — and clamped down hard on my feelings, though it was the more difficult thing to do. In time — in its own good time — the pit had simply disappeared, given way to ordinary daylight and the events of a lifetime. Nor had the voice ever returned.

Perhaps my father would have said that that had been a vision. Others, had I told them, might have said that hearing voices was symptomatic of schizophrenia. Far worse, far more frightening, had been my experience aboard ship where I had subsequently spent two years aboard a carrier, the *Hornet.*

I had been a yeoman in the gunnery division of the ship during the early 'fifties, after high school and before college. The gunnery bridge, which was where I had my battle station, was on the next level above the Captain's bridge. It had been an interesting place to be. If I weren't there officially — that is, if I weren't at my battle station with my headphones on — I could watch "air ops" or refueling operations and eavesdrop on the Captain and the Executive Officer.

One day I was leaning over the inboard rail beside my friend Chief Gunner Adams as the planes were landing and being recovered. As one particular plane was coming in a hugely strange sensation billowed out of my heart; it was comprised of excitement and anticipation, and it riveted my eyes on the aircraft. I knew it was going to crash.

When the plane — a Corsair — touched down, the right hand landing gear collapsed. The plane slued sideways and headed for the island. Gunner Adams yelled, "Duck!" and hit the deck, but I just stood looking down, fascinated. The Corsair smashed into the island exactly beneath my feet. A wing took most of the force of the collision. It crumpled. The air crewmen were all over the plane immediately, hosing it down, covering it with foam, hauling the pilot out of the cockpit — he was unhurt.

Gunner Adams got to his feet cursing. "Jesus," he said. "You could've been sprayed with burning gas." He brushed himself off looking both angry and chagrined. I said nothing, but it occurred to me that if I had been covered with burning gasoline, so would the gunner lying on the deck at my feet.

The very next time I watched air ops it happened again. The same feeling, the same knowledge. This time it was one of the light bombers they called "Turkeys." Like the Corsair, it was a prop plane. As it came in over the flight deck it appeared to be in perfect position for a landing. Its hook was dangling from its tail, ready to grab the cables that stretched athwart the deck, but at the last moment the *Hornet*'s stern slid down a swell and the plane was fifteen or twenty feet in the air instead of touching down. It fell, the deck rose up again, and the plane bounced. So did the landing hook, missing all three of the cables. The Turkey smashed nose-first into the planes that had landed earlier and been spotted on the bow, waiting for the elevators to take them down to the hangar deck.

That pilot had not been hurt, either, much to my relief. I was beginning to wonder whether my presence had anything to do with the crashes, for there had been no others during the cruise except those I'd been watching. Perhaps I was a jinx. But that was superstitious and egocentric.

The third time it was a jet. The day was perfect — the sea was calm, the winds were steady. The *Hornet* lay upon the ocean as though it were built into the water. As the airplane approached the fantail I felt the same emotions, excitement and anticipation, as I had on the two previous occasions, but a third had been added: immense fear.

I was unable to move any part of my body excepting my head and eyes. I knew that this plane, too, was going to crash, but that this time the pilot would die.

I was relieved and elated to know, when the jet touched down, that I wasn't prescient after all. The landing hook grabbed the first cable and the plane was stretched to a stop, the spotter lifted his flags and began to direct the pilot to his parking place forward.

I looked away to see the next plane land. As I did so, I heard a terrible, squealing noise. I looked back to see the plane that had just landed going over the port side. I saw the tail tilt into the air as the nose headed down along the hull. Anguish filled me. The plane's engine had failed to cut off, and it had pushed the aircraft over the rail. I could see the tire marks scribed across the flight deck by the brake-locked wheels. I couldn't see the end of the crash, but I was told later that when the plane had hit the water it had tipped over on the cockpit, trapping the pilot inside, and sunk in the open sea before anyone could get to it.

If these were "visions," I wanted no part of them. If they were religious experiences of any kind, they did not indicate the existence of a loving god, the Lord that my father cherished against all the evidence of my senses and my experience; rather, they indicated, perhaps, that I myself was the "god" who was dreaming this world, and the dreams were dark, terrifying, sorrowful dreams. For my sanity's sake, I rejected this possibility and kept it as far out of my consciousness as I could. But I never watched air ops again. There were no more crashes while I was aboard.

I'd had no other remarkable experiences for more than a year. By then I had been transferred to Arlington, Virginia, just outside Washington, D. C., and I was working at the Bureau of Naval Personnel. It was the last year of my enlistment, and I had been transformed into a mythical being, not because of what had happened aboard the *Hornet,* for I had told no one about my foresights, but because I worked in the Shore Duty Section of the Bureau and was, in fact, the yeoman who worked on the list itself, filling out and filing cards for those sailors who wanted to come ashore and spend at least part of their enlistments on land. Though no one at sea might know my name, everyone in the fleet thought about The Shore Duty Yeoman all the time.

I was often visited by bo'sun's mates and gunner's mates, deck ratings that had little chance of obtaining a shore billet, for there were many of them with years at sea and few things for them to do on the beach. I would feel very bad for them when they asked what their chances were. I would shake my head, show them the number of cards between the number-one man on the list and their position in the file, and when they asked, "When would you say?" I would reply, "Not for another three years," perhaps, or four, or five. And they would swear and ask me how much of a bribe it would require to get their cards moved up.

At that juncture my stomach would wrench itself into a knot of pain and I would send the sailor on his way with no hope. Then I would reach into my drawer for the bottle of pink fluid and see that it was empty again. I would make my way to sickbay and hand my bottle across the counter to the medic on duty who would go to a demijohn of the pink fluid and fill the bottle from a spigot. Before I went back to my filing tubs I would take a swig — I had long since stopped trying to measure the stuff out. By the time I got back to my post the knot would have untied itself. I would find years later, through an x-ray photograph, that I'd had an ulcer in those days, an ulcer that had eventually healed itself.

When I got back to my filing tubs I would sit down and begin to work. And then I would have an out-of-body experience. If those had been the 'sixties instead of the mid-'fifties, I would have known that I was an addict, and that the wraith that lifted itself out of my mind and hovered above my body, looking down at me as I worked, had been produced by a drug-induced hallucination. As it was, I did not know, and when I was discharged I had experienced no withdrawal symptoms at all. Getting married and laboring with my father-in-law building houses during the summer had cured my ulcer without my being medicated or hospitalized.

Here was a case in which the Watcher had clearly been oneself, not my father's Other. But how can a drug release the spirit from the body and set it floating overhead? How can there be two sets of the same eyes, one looking at the names on endless stacks of cards, the other looking at the back of the head that holds those eyes? I could not deny that it was a mystery, but I accepted mystery as an element of life, though I always assumed that there was a reasonable explanation for everything, even though I might not know what that explanation could be. It was like mathematics: I knew it existed, but I understood very little about it.

In 1968 I awoke one Sunday morning and knew my father, whom I loved despite everything, was in peril of his life. I phoned home from Potsdam, New York, where I was a visiting professor for the year. "Promise me that you won't shovel the sidewalk this winter," I said, uneasily assuming that this labor was the threat, for father was seventy-eight years old, after all, and, though he had walked everywhere all his life, since he had retired from his pastorate he had become relatively sedentary. After some bandying of words father had agreed not to exert himself unduly.

On the following Wednesday he was dead. He had been watching the news on television when he pitched forward into darkness or light.

When I went back for the funeral mother told me, "He didn't like his high blood pressure medicine. He said it made him dizzy, so he wouldn't take it." My telepathic message had been imprecise, or at least as ambiguous as the epitaph I put on my father's grave: "The good man is gone; pray his eyes see now what his heart saw."

I saw no reason to disbelieve in telepathy. It was very likely a natural phenomenon, like radio waves. Augury was another thing, however, so that this incident and the problem with the crashing airplanes caused me some worry. At last I worked it out philosophically to my satisfaction when I ran across the ancient symbol of Ouroboros, the snake that devours its own tail. It was supposed to be an alchemical sign as well, the Hermetic Dragon. The image in which it was drawn I understood to be inexact, for the universe was at least three dimensional, not a two-dimensional circle, but I had no argument with the concept of the self-destroying, self-perpetuating universe. I even saw some scientific evidence for it in the so-called "black holes" the cosmologists had discovered in space, where matter and energy were evidently disappearing. No doubt they were reappearing "on the other side."

I, who had always had a deep fear of death, found solace in the idea that the universe was, is, and always shall be. I found it easier to believe that this was so than that some supernatural being existed on the same terms, which only begged the question. If the end was in the beginning and the beginning in the end, as the religious doctrines of the world had always maintained, then it was conceivable to me that the cosmos might even be evolving a godhead out of itself — in other words, that the universe might be willing itself to consciousness through evolution, and that once this had been done, then "God" would exist and "He" would be not only "in" all things, he would *be* all things.

Or, as my favorite poet and friend Howard Nemerov had put it in his epigram "Creation Myth on a Mobius Strip,"

This world's just mad enough to have been made
By the Being His beings into Being prayed.

This is what I meant when I remarked in conversations that I was by no means an atheist, nor even an agnostic; that I had been raised a Baptist, but am now a Cosmist. Obviously, however, since evolution was still taking place, the Universe had not yet gotten to the point of Godhead.

None of these metaphysical manipulations, however, did me much good when I contemplated personal physical and mental extinction. That was no doubt why my mind or, to be specific, my neo-cortex, provided me with the experience of death through a dream-vision.

I had been fascinated to read Arthur Koestler on the subject of the three minds of human beings: the upper spinal node or "reptile brain," which is in charge of involuntary bodily functions such as the heartbeat; the hypothalamus or "mammal brain," which cannot think but provides us with feelings and reactions, and the neo-cortex or strictly "human brain," which is rational and conscious, but has no feelings. This latter brain had evolved so fast, according to Koestler and his sources, that it has few neural connections with the lower brains on which it rests uneasily. "Ah!" it says when it sees a dead sparrow, "that sparrow is dead." And farther down the street the neo-cortex says, "Oh, and that squirrel is dead, too." And a bit further along, "Hmmm, and here is a dead dog." After a bit of cogitation it says, "Well, since I am also an animal, my life is finite and I will eventually also be dead."

Panic beneath the neo-cortex! The horse brain feels a threat from above. How to escape — there is no way! Although, of course, being unable to think, it does not put such "thoughts" into "words." But now the neo-cortex is posed with a dilemma: how to coexist with such a constantly panic-stricken entity as the hypothalamus? "I know," the upper brain says, "I will invent art, philosophy, music, literature and religion in order to pacify it. I will tell it that it will live forever in a never-never land somewhere to the east of Erewhon. And I will invent science and mathematics for myself."

So I dreamt one night that I was an attendant in a gas station in a poor location. It was shadowed, even in daylight. The cars drove past now and then on their great tires — for some reason the time period was the late 'twenties or early 'thirties, but there weren't many on the road in this part of the city.

Evening was coming on, darkness moving in. There was an air of something waiting in the corners of the station, in the gas pumps, behind the cooler. It was summer. If the lights were on perhaps someone might turn off the road, drive up the old macadam, ride over the sparse grass in the cracks, stop there, outside the dusty window where I stood waiting. Then, with the thought, they were there, four of them getting out of the square sedan.

As they came filing toward the door, heads turned, looking at me through the grimy glass with their hard eyes, I knew there was no way out. They'll find no money, though — something in me grinned at the thought, and the thought worried me.

They were staring at me. The first was nearly at the door. As our eyes locked I was shocked by the pistol in this stranger's hand, by the flame in the muzzle, the shattered glass, by my blindness as the bullet entered the brain where I knew I was lost and reeling, blood pouring between my fingers clutching my head, bathing my eyes, and no sensation of pain, only . . . a vague regret that I would now accomplish no more; certainty that this was death; amazement that I could think with a shattered brain; knowledge that if I woke again they would have saved me; rejection of the possibility.

But beyond these thoughts and sensations, and above them, there was an overriding sensation of euphoria, of immense joy. It was over. Death was nothing — nothing I could have imagined; mere joy, great relief, release, and silence.

When I awoke I could not at first believe in waking. The incident hadn't happened, yet nothing more real had ever happened to me. Stumbling out of my blood into the walking dream of life, nothing was left except the evening with its images of weed and dust, flame in a dark cylinder, and joy. And from that moment on I had not feared death, though it could not be said that I looked forward to it.

In this case, obviously, I had not been merely an observer, but the main participant. The only participant, if one considers that the gunman and his friends were merely figments, actors conjured out of the web of dream for the purpose of the vision, which was surely to convince my hypothalamus that the act of dying was positively pleasurable, even when bloody violence was involved. What a clever creature was this human brain which contained a universe of characters and situations within itself!

Was this the sort of vision my father had always wished to have and been denied? I doubted it. Was it the sort my mother had had when she was a girl? Not likely, though her stories of living in Chicago during the days of Al Capone might have given my neo-cortex its scenario. She claimed to have been living in an apartment directly above a spot on the street where a mob hit had taken place.

If I had never consciously desired to experience a vision of any kind, I had always wanted to see a ghost, although to do so would have destroyed my theories about the Hereafter or, rather, the lack thereof. And then one day I did, although "experiencing" would be a more accurate word to describe the event than "seeing."

It had been necessary one winter for me to go for four weeks to stay in Louisville, a city several hundred miles from my Oswego, New York, home. When I arrived I found that I was to live on the second floor of a house whose owner was in the hospital temporarily with back problems. I settled in as best I could, but when I wanted to go into the bathroom I felt repelled. Cold fear caught at my throat — there was no other way to describe it except in those hackneyed terms. Since I had no choice except to go in, I found the pull-string on the light over the mirror as quickly as possible and pulled it.

When the light went on I found that it was an old-fashioned room with no shower, only a vast tub, a lavatory, and a stool. The room gave me the willies, and it was exceedingly cold. I could not imagine running water in the tub and taking a bath, though that would eventually be necessary. I finished my business and got out as quickly as I could. Thereafter, whenever I had to use those facilities at night I would stand at the door, lean in as far as I could, and pull the light on before I would enter.

It was friends of the landlord who told me later that a young man had committed suicide by lying in the tub and slicing his wrists, bleeding to death in the warm water. None of my theories was able to explain this phenomenon, which flew in the face of my old friend Ouroboros, the Hermetic Dragon, but it had been as real to me as my dream of dying. Perhaps violent death etches an emotional "photograph" on its surroundings — that was as good an explanation as I could come up with, though it is rather lame.

I had no explanation at all for the true vision when it occurred. I had driven my wife to the beauty parlor for a haircut one glorious autumn afternoon in Oswego. I had been waiting for her in the car, which had been parked on a strip beside the building which was located on a hillside in a residential neighborhood. I had been enjoying the fine day, staring in particular at a tree that was full of fall colors. Suddenly a tingling sensation raced along my spine, then radiated throughout my body. I knew I was going to experience a vision, though I had never had one before. "Oh, no," I said to myself, "am I really?"

And while I looked at the tree I was suddenly in two "places" at once. The first place was in the midst of life — unthinking life, which had willed itself out of nothingness. The other place was in that nothingness itself. I was in the midst of an oblivion that was absolute: there was nothing outside it, and there was nothing within it.

It was an impossibility for me to be in those two places, for the one obviated the other, canceled it out. Nothingness could contain nothing which might will itself into existence, and life was not a force which willed itself into being, it was simply itself, not conscious in any way. But I stared at the tree and there I was, in two places at once, in the midst of life and nothingness.

The vision didn't last long. When it faded I was still sitting in my car on a glorious autumn afternoon, waiting for Jean.

And now, here I am, sitting on the living room floor, my work-glove on my right hand, Seeger wrapped around it, biting my thumb, raking my palm with his hind claws. It is a strange time to think of the quotation I ran across in John Cheever's *Journals,* but there it is in my mind as I wrestle with my cat:

"We rise from sleep all natural men, boisterous, loving, and hopeful, but the dark-faced stranger is waiting at the door, the viper is coiled in the garden, the old man whispers lewdly to the boy, and the woman sits at her table crying."

"Bravo!" says the voice behind me, but I don't turn to look. I have faith that No One is there.

THE VIEW FROM A WINTER GARRETT

A Discussion by T. L. Ponick, Editor, *The Edge City Review*

Skies are gray and winter is settling down
Past my attic window as I write.
I see my neighbors' roofs adrift through town

Blown by the wind winding them in white.
The current of my mind begins to spill
Into a fault of time. I watch a flight

Of gulls come rising out of chimneys, fill
A fold of sky that falls in siftings there
Into Ontario below the hill.

I hear the wind build palaces of air
And ice along the shore of Whitman's lake.
Only silence will make a dwelling where

Music must turn to crystal to survive,
And seagulls scull like snowfall come alive.

This is generally the kind of poem we don't favor in *Edge City Review,* a poem about the inner feelings of the writer/poet, which, in this case, conjoin the artist's thoughts to the imagery of a cold, wintry day in the Great Lakes region — which is about as cold and wintry as you can get. And yet, after describing an almost conventionally bleak outdoor scene, Turco snaps the reader to attention in his concluding three lines:

Only silence will make a dwelling where

Music must turn to crystal to survive,
And seagulls scull like snowfall come alive.

While the concluding couplet can survive on its own, its stand-alone meaning is further augmented by the preceding line which turns a pair of pure but related images into a profound observation on the connection of poetry and art to nature. Further, although in modern idiom, the images are nearly Wordsworthian in their simple grandeur, particularly the last one in which we see snowflakes morph into seagulls rowing powerfully against the currents of the wind, each like a miniature crew-shell of one. The final line is loaded as well with icy "s" sounds carrying over from the previous line's "survive," an old poetical trick, but one made new again with more modern imagery. Turco's poem is simple but elegant. It doesn't engage as strongly as [some], but it gives us an epiphany of time and place that remains long after we have read the poem — the kind of pleasurable effect that fans of John Ashbery will never know.

THE HOUSE OF DREAMS

It was amazingly cold for what I had conceived of as a southern city. I had arrived in Louisville a day earlier and lodged in the home of a faculty member of the University of Louisville where I was to be Bingham Poet-in-residence for four weeks early in 1982. The weather then had been normally chilly, but the room in the apartment I was to use was very hot and stuffy, and the door had to be left open in order for the unusual heating system to work properly, a fact that meant I would be sleeping with the cats of the household. I loved cats, but I didn't sleep even with my own assortment in Upstate New York. Had I known that the temperature would plunge to twenty below zero and stay there for an unconscionable period, I would not have changed my residence.

But another place was available for me to use: a room on the second floor of a house belonging to Shirley Williams, a woman journalist who, unfortunately, had hurt her back and was at the moment in the hospital. A fellow roomer, a young man named Max, lived on the ground floor. He let me in and helped me carry my bags upstairs to a room full of windows made of uninsulated glass that let in the January cold with no resistance at all.

I had congratulated myself, as I left Syracuse airport, on escaping a month of Lake Ontario winter, at the same time that I'd felt guilty about leaving my family to fend for itself while I basked in the comfort of a mild Kentucky winter during my college's "inter-session" between Christmas and the beginning of the spring term. "I guess I don't have to feel quite so guilty," I said to the image in the mirror over the golden oak dresser against the wall. Framed there I saw the picture of a visiting professor, middle-aged, heavy with the years that I'd let slip by without taking much care of myself. I'd already given up my pipe, and soon I'd have to go on a diet as well.

I decided not to change my clothes for dinner with Sue and Leon Driskell who lived only two blocks away in this neighborhood of settled homes not far off Bardstown Road. It was too cold, and I was already feeling forlorn. I had the second floor entirely to myself. "No doubt I'll feel better once I begin to teach," I said. I wished I'd brought a pipe and tobacco. I glanced at my watch and noted that Leon Driskell would be arriving at any moment to pick me up.

I went into the hall and walked toward the bathroom to comb my hair and wash my hands. When I got to the door I stopped and peered inside, into the darkness of the early winter evening. My stopping puzzled me. The hall was cold, but not nearly so cold as the air that breathed out of the bathroom. I shuddered involuntarily, said to myself, "This is ridiculous," and reached through the door to grope for the light switch — there was none.

I had to step through the doorway to find the pull-cord on the fixture above the mirror over the sink. My image in the glass, appearing suddenly, startled me. I glanced about — there was no shower, only a large, old-fashioned tub. I hated the thought of having to bathe in it in such weather. I combed hurriedly and left the room as soon I could.

I met my academic host at the front door, which was located at the foot of the stairway, in a hall filled with pictures of literary lights and artists of all kinds — photographs, caricatures, sketches. "I apologize for Louisville," Driskell said. We walked through the wind to his house where I met Sue, his wife, and settled down before the fireplace with drinks.

"What a relief!" I said. "That house is cold. I hope the weather breaks soon."

Leon apologized again. "This is very unusual for Louisville," he said.

Sue passed some cheese and crackers on a ceramic plate she had made in her shop-studio further downtown, which I would subsequently visit. She was pleasant and homey, an artist, not an academic herself. I felt comfortable with her — with both of them, in different ways. "I guess it's going to continue this way for a while," she said, "according to the weather reports."

"And I had my choice between this time and later in the spring!" I laughed. "This was more convenient. But I'm always making the wrong choice whenever I do something like this — not that I do it so often." I took a piece of cheese and a cracker.

"It's unfortunate that Beverly's in the hospital with her ruptured disk," Leon said, "but how do you like the house?"

"It's interesting," I replied. "It has two furnaces, one of which is evidently broken down; there's no insulation at all, and it's impossible to keep the temperature up even to sixty, according to my house mate. But if the rest of the house is cold, it's nothing compared to the upstairs bathroom which is bone-cold somehow." I noticed that Leon and Sue exchanged startled glances, but at the moment I passed it off.

After dinner we had a discussion about dreams and I told them about a dream I'd had a few nights before I'd left to come to Louisville, a dream that had embarrassed me. It hadn't been embarrassing because it was a sex dream. It embarrassed me because it was so trite. Thinking about it later on I realized that a psychoanalyst would interpret it to mean that I was neurotic or worse, but as a writer I understood that once something was recorded it belonged to the audience as much as to its creator, so the analyst would be entitled to his or her opinion.

"Psychoanalysis is nothing more than literary criticism anyway," I said to the Driskells — Leon was a critic himself. "After all, how much of a dream does one remember once he wakes up? A half? A third? Less? And in what order is it recollected — the same as that in which it was dreamed? Does one remember all of it at once, or does one have to think about it and call up the details by sheer willpower?" I had done that back in New York State not long ago with another dream I had thoroughly enjoyed and wanted to keep, to make conscious so that I could keep it. But how many of those details had I invented after I was awake, in order to provide my mind with a continuity acceptable to a sense of logic or order?

"So when one tells someone a dream it's second hand to the narrator and third hand to the listener. In other words," I said, "you're telling your listener a story. You're doing nothing different from what a writer does as he is writing. If one happens to be lying on a psychiatrist's office couch, maybe the analyst is writing it down or taping it and it will show up later in a book, just like any other short story.

"And that's why I'm not interested in deep analysis," I continued. "I'd just as soon have my dream reviewed by Gene Shallit on the *Today* show, or maybe deliver it as a paper at an academic conference on 'Deconstructivist Hermeneutics and the Deep Image in Dreamscape,' then let a panel of my colleagues chew it to death. Freud and his friends did nothing more or less than what writers and critics have been doing since words were invented."

Leon nodded his head. "It's true," he said. "Writers were the first psychologists. Their interest is in character and the human condition — people and their reactions to the situations in which they find themselves."

"That's why I was embarrassed by the dream I'd like to forget," I said. It had been as bad as watching television. I couldn't conjure up all the trivial details, for I had consciously tried to suppress them, but I could still call to mind the broad outline:

A man had been murdered and most of his body found, all of it excepting one arm. It was clearly supposed to be a terrifying dream, and it was apparent to me even in the dream that everything hinged on that missing arm. I could recall understanding that I would eventually run across the arm; everything else between the discovery of the body and then of the arm was filler.

That was when I began to feel embarrassed, or at least sheepish and uneasy. I and another character in the dream were moving, or we were at a used clothing emporium, or something of the sort. I had no very clear idea of who the other main character was. It may have been another child, like myself, who was simultaneously an adult. Sometimes I thought the other child was Phil Reilly, the boy who had lived across the street from me in the fifth and sixth grades. Phil had a mongoloid brother of whom I had been afraid. Sometimes I thought it was my own brother Gene with whom I had been moved all over town by our parents when we were children. They had been on a pilgrimage in search of the Perfect Landlord, or at least a place that was respectable that they could afford. At any rate, in the dream I and the other character were packing clothes into boxes.

It was my playmate who discovered the arm lying among the discarded articles of clothing. At this point in the dream I had realized that I was supposed to feel terrified, and I recalled trying to work up a good terror, but all I had managed was a slightly disgusted feeling. I assumed I was disgusted both with the predictability of the dream and with the device of the arm. However, there they all were in the middle of a miserable excuse for a nightmare, and I had felt they had to go on with it and get it over with.

My playmate at this point had stuck the arm into a plastic garbage bag and begun to chase me with it. I fled shrieking as I was supposed to do, but I still couldn't get particularly upset except with the dream itself. I felt something had to be done to jazz up the plot, so I had my playmate (or brother) throw the arm at me, but it had missed by a good distance. The arm fell out of the bag and lay on the ground. It began to twitch. It was alive. Naturally.

The Driskells laughed.

I had become completely disgusted with the whole proceeding. "My id, or whatever was 'controlling' this production, at this point came up with something totally bizarre in a desperate attempt to save the narrative." I paused.

"'It called you 'Daddy,'" I had said to my playmate derisively, nausea knotting up my stomach. God, this is bad! I had thought.

The Driskells laughed again and Sue refilled my cup.

"If my playmate were my brother, and the arm were my brother's offspring, then that made me the uncle of an arm." I shook my head as the Driskells responded with more laughter. Outraged to have allowed such a revoltingly bad fantasy to usurp my night, I had taken myself by the scruff of the dream and shaken myself, shaken myself awake and lain there listening to the stained glass clock ticking to itself in the darkness.

What had I been doing sleeping up in the attic with its kneewall down both sides of the room, filled with shelves of books? While my wife and son (my daughter grown and gone) lay sleeping on the second floor below, the screen of the computer dark at the end of the room?

I had lain listening to silence filling up my hollow bones, trying one last time to feel a twinge of terror, but there was nothing terrifying in that semi-old house, not even in the attic study or in the semi-old college town, nothing frightening even in my constant knowledge that I was growing old, that I might die, at any beat, of a heart attack or a stroke. I had listened to my son cough once or twice downstairs, and I had heard my wife cough as well, as though in answer — that was what I had been doing sleeping on a cot in the attic study. I had been trying not to catch the winter flu, at least not while I had to care for my sick family.

"And now here I am," I said sipping my coffee, "in Louisville later on in the coldest winter on record, living in an unheated house, afraid to go into the bathroom because it is twice as cold as any other room in the place." Again the Driskells looked at each other. "What's wrong?" I asked.

At last they told me. "A teen-aged boy committed suicide in that bathroom," Leon said. "He slit his wrists and lay in the warm bathtub until they found him," Sue added.

When I got back to the house after the evening of dinner and good fellowship, I stood in the frigid bathroom and stared at the tub. I was still incredulous. "My job is to be imaginative, but at heart I am a practical man," I said to the man in the mirror. I had never put credence in ghost stories, though I liked to read them well enough. Nevertheless, I had no doubt that I felt something in the room, something left over, a shadow of despair. While I stood in the bathroom I dreamt another dream, a daydream this time. I imagined the details that the Driskells had not known:

The boy came into the house from school, letting himself in with his own key. His parents were still away — the car was gone from the driveway, and their coats were missing from the hallseat. He put his books down on it and stood for a moment, thinking of what he would do. He couldn't bear, at the moment, to remember Gloria handing him back his pin in Mr. Clancy's chemistry class, wrapped in a scented note folded into a scented pink envelope. That had been the longest class of his life, but when it was over things had gotten even worse. Unbidden, against his will, the image of Gloria rose to memory — he saw her going through the door hugging her texts to her breast, the arm of Johnny Martin around her waist. She hadn't glanced back, but Johnny had, and his grin had been smug and triumphant.

He stood in the hall a while longer until his eyes refocused and he realized that he was looking into the single picture hanging on the wall. It was a landscape, the vista of an ideal country. There were hills and a lake, sheep grazing in a meadow, a piper playing silences to a shepherdess. He recalled the poem they had been studying in English class, Keats' "Ode to a Grecian Urn." He couldn't bring to mind the exact lines the picture recalled to him, so he bent to his books and picked up the textbook the class had been reading. He found what he was looking for on page 101: "Bold Lover, never, never canst thou kiss, / Though winning near the goal — yet, do not grieve; / She cannot fade, though thou hast not thy bliss, / for ever wilt thou love, and she be fair!"

He hadn't understood the poem at first, but Mr. Haskins had explained it, and he understood it now. He wished he could freeze time at yesterday when Gloria had still been his. He'd have settled for that.

He turned around and saw the mail lying where it had fallen through the slot onto the floor of the hall and been pushed to one side when he came in. It lay on the carpet, near the edge against the wall. He went over and picked up the stack, began to thumb through it. His hand froze when he read the return address on one of the envelopes. His fingers trembled slightly, and he thought he detected the faint stirrings of excitement, even of hope, but he suspended the moment of discovery while he went into the dining room and sat down at the table. He picked up a clean knife left over from breakfast and slit the envelope.

He read what the letter said, but the words wouldn't sink into his consciousness at first. It was from his father's Alma Mater, and when at last he allowed himself to understand, he realized that he was now utterly undone — the college had refused to accept him for admission in the coming fall. How could he countenance this? How could he face his father?

And then the weight of the world fell upon him. His shoulders slumped with it, the air went white before his vision. He could hear the clock ticking on the mantel, each swing of the pendulum pushing isolate sounds toward him, the walls magnifying them rather than drinking them in.

He sat a while listening to the clock, to the noise of an occasional automobile passing in the street, to the counterpoint of his heart. At last it all drained away, leaving a clear, cool space, and he got up. He went into the hall and up the stairs.

He went into the bathroom and bent to the tub. While the water was running into it he stripped and stood shivering in the chill air. He bent forward, leaned on the sink, and stared at the face that gazed out of the mirror. There was nothing to see beyond the flesh — the eyes were dark and the hair, the skin was pale and ordinary, like the features. He felt nothing about them except a vague distaste.

In the cabinet there was his father's strop razor. He picked it off the shelf and carried it to the tub. Stepping over the rim, he first tested the water, then lowered himself into it. He lay still for a while, decided to leave the taps running. He lifted the razor, opened it, and laid the edge across his wrist.

One strong movement was all it took, and one on the other wrist. He dropped the razor onto the floor and closed his eyes. He didn't open them to see the bright red eddies rising to color the sweet waves that flooded over him as the tide ebbed.

In bed that evening I lay and attempted to recapture another dream I had had not long before the grade B production about the arm, the chaotic dream that was without plot, without characterization, with little recognizable theme, but full of atmosphere. I had been back in the now decaying town of my childhood, seeing it from an angle I had never experienced before. I had been searching for my wife, who had also grown up in that old New England city, and I had run across quaking ditches in the backyard of an abandoned house to get to the huge roses made of straw that were blooming in the front yard.

But also in the front yard there was a man growing up out of the ground on a stem that extended itself as I watched, and when it flowered the man began to fly. I, the watcher, thought, "I'll try to soar too," and I did try, but, though I couldn't manage much more than a brief great hop, still the feeling of joy was overwhelming in my breast, joy in all that decay and those bogs of delicious rust and my wife and children lost somewhere in the buildings that were nothing more than shells of stone filled with debris; there was only joy in the dusty attic filled with darkness and music and the words of books crowding each other upon the silent shelves.

THE LAMENT OF TURKO THE TERRIBLE

The inspiration for much of what I write is what I read, as I discussed at the beginning of this book when I spoke about Margaret Mead's image of the ". . . world of the first rose, and the first lark's song" and the genesis of my poem "Dawn Song." In fact, I have written entire books based on other people's writing, such as *The Compleat Melancholick,* which is subtitled, "A Sequence of Found, Composite, and Composed Poems Based Largely upon Robert Burton's [English Renaissance tome] *The Anatomy of Melancholy*" and *Emily Dickinson, Woman of Letters,* which is comprised mainly of a sequence of poems titled "A Sampler of Hours: Poems and Centos from Lines in Emily Dickinson's Letters."

This habit is one of the reasons (though perhaps not the main reason) why I stopped reading, and never finished, James Joyce's *Ulysses,* for when I ran across this passage containing my name, (though misspelled with a "k" rather than a "c") — "She heard old Royce sing in the pantomime of Turko the terrible and laughed with others when he sang, 'I am the boy / That can enjoy / Invisibility,'" I had to stop and write this lament:

Some folk call me Turko,
Turko the terrible Turk.
James Joyce wrote about me
Through some fantastic quirk —
For he could not know of me,
Since I had not been born.
Still, he'd the sense to counsel
The ages and to warn

That I'd appear
To strain your ear
And hospitality:
I am the boy
That can enjoy
Invisibility.

I have been pantomiming
Now over forty years,

Scribbling and inditing
So much you'd think the tears
Of editors and readers
Would swamp the Muses' boat.
But no, not even Turko
Can sink it — it will float

Down Moby's road
Despite my load
Of inability.
I am the boy
That can enjoy
Invisibility.

What's fine about my singing
Is not my crackling voice,
But that, though I go inkling,
The world still has its choice,
Like Royce, to miss or laugh at
The witless fogs I pen.
The stars, they go on spinning;
The Earth now and again

Churns as I sing,
And fall and spring
At things as they may be.
I am the boy
That can enjoy
Invisibility.

HOW I GOT INTO BOOKS

On occasion I've been asked how I came to be involved in bookselling, let alone book writing and criticizing, but I have actually been involved with books on various levels all of my life, so there was no transition of any kind from one thing to another. Though my family, like nearly everyone else, had no money during the Depression, our home was full of books of all sorts. My mother read to me from the cradle, and I soon learned to read for myself. Nor was writing a mysterious act, because every week for as long as I can remember I watched my father hunched over his typewriter hunting out and pecking at his weekly sermons.

I began to collect books myself as soon as I could read, and I enjoyed reading so much that I very early decided that I wanted to be a writer, to my parents' sorrow, for they wanted me to be a Bible thumper. Although that was not to be my destiny, like my father while he wrote his sermons I was soon bent over our sturdy old manual typewriter hunting and pecking out short stories and verses.

At Suffield Academy in Suffield, Connecticut, which I attended during the eighth and ninth grades, I wrote articles and poems for the school paper, *The Bell,* and when I was fifteen in 1949, just before I transferred to Meriden High School, one of my short stories won third prize in a summertime high school fiction contest. My tale was published with the other winners by the sponsor, one of the two local newspapers in Meriden, Connecticut. In high school I was clippings librarian (called the "morgue clerk") and cub reporter for *The Morning Record,* which eventually absorbed the afternoon paper, *The Journal,* for which I had been a delivery boy beginning in the fifth grade and continuing until I went to Suffield. *The Record-Journal* later, after I'd spent a four-year hitch in the Navy, gave me two undergraduate scholarships to attend the University of Connecticut, which very nicely augmented the G. I. Bill.

My seventh-grade shop teacher, John Houdlette of Lincoln Junior High School In Meriden had a daughter, Jean Houdlette, whom I had noticed early on. In high school we were classmates, and we were members of the same crowd. Some of the boys in that crowd started a science-fiction reading club called The Fantaseers which supported a one-bookcase library at my house — in 2004 I published a book titled *Fantaseers, A Book of Memories*; there is a photo of the

Fantaseers' library in it. By the time we graduated, of course, all those books were left behind and became part of my own collection. By the time Jean and I were married in 1956 I had books everywhere and no place to put them, so I brought a lot of them up to Jean's family place in Dresden, Maine, adding them to the large collection that was already there. They were like snow: over the years they accumulated in drifts.

In 1960 I began teaching English literature and creative writing at Fenn College, now Cleveland State University, and over the years since then I've written a great many book manuscripts, fifty of which have appeared in print. However, it was a late colleague of mine at the State University of New York College at Oswego, where I directed the Program in Writing Arts and taught for 31 years, who got me started as a bookseller. His name was David Winslow. He had a PhD in folklore, but he had had several other careers as well, including selling antiques and books. He taught me what I know about books as a commodity when he and I, on weekends mostly, became what are known as "book scouts." We would sell the books we found upstate to downstate New York book dealers. And, of course, I also sold some of the books I had been accumulating.

One day David called me up to say that there was a big sale of stuff in Hannibal, not far from Oswego. He said that they'd advertised books, but when we got there all we found of books was a box of paperbacks under one table. Dave sneered and walked away to look at other things, but I went through the paperbacks and found one, a first edition paperback original titled *My Hope for America* by Lyndon Baines Johnson. I bought it for ten cents.

When we got back to the car Dave saw that I'd bought something, asked to see it, and then began to rag me about it. All I'd paid for it was a dime, but he acted as though I'd thrown away a fortune. By the time we got back to my house I was furious and had decided that I would wreak my revenge.

My mother had been good with handicrafts, and she had taught me how to bind a book. In college I had bound my paperback textbooks so that they'd last longer, and as an adult I had taken to binding paperbacks and restoring old books as a hobby, so I took the Johnson book, quarter-bound it in cloth and leather, put it in a package with an old leather-bound hymnal, and sent it with return postage to former President Lyndon Johnson. In an enclosed letter I asked him if he would be willing to sign my book in exchange for the hymnal, which I hoped he would accept as a gift.

Not a great while after that I got the book back. President Johnson had signed a Presidential bookplate for me, and he included a letter on official stationery telling me that he was delighted with the hymnal, which he was going to place in the L. B. J. Presidential Library in Texas. I pasted the bookplate onto the inside-front cover of *My Hope for America,* and I tipped his letter into the volume. Then I called David and asked him to come over to the house so that I could show him a book I had picked up for ten cents at a lousy sale in Hannibal. Later on, I sold the book for a lot of money on one of our downstate book trips.

On another of those trips Dave took me to a book dealer in Johnstown, New York, where I was shown an old book that had no cover page, and it was missing some other pages as well. At the time I was collecting books and doing research for a book manuscript I would soon write titled *Satan's Scourge: A Narrative of the Age of Witchcraft in England and New England 1580–1697.* I thought I knew what the book was that the dealer had shown me, despite its lack of a title page, so I bought it for $25.00. When I got it home I looked it up and sure enough, it was a first edition copy of *A True and Faithful Relation of What Passed for Many Years Between Dr. John Dee and Some Spirits,* etc., edited, with a Preface, by Meric. Casaubon, and published in London in 1659.

Dr. Dee was Royal Mathematician to Queen Elizabeth I, but he was also interested in spiritual matters. The book I had found is one of the most famous occult books in the English language. It was a record of the conversations William Kelly, Dr. Dee's con-man pal, had with Madimi and many other celestial beings, as he dictated them to the good Doctor who could see and hear nothing in the crystal Kelly used. Kelly came to a bad end. My wife and I saw Dr. Dee's crystal ball — it was egg-shaped, really — in the British Museum while we were in England in 1993.

I wrote to the Cornell University Library, which has a great occult collection, and asked them to send me photocopies of the missing pages. I then restored it and hand-bound it in studded, leather-covered wooden boards in 1971. Many years later, after I had finished my own book, begun the Mathom Bookshop in Dresden, and gone on-line, I sold that book to someone in Australia for $1000.00.

During our summers in Maine I would go out on bookfinding trips, sometimes alone, sometimes with Jean, and sometimes her sister Nathalie would come along. One of the places we would go to find books was Frank McQuaid's Book Barn in Edgecomb. He had been a World War II bomber pilot, and I had been a sailor during and after the Korean War. We held similar political views, so often he and I would sit around gabbing, and then he began to take me out on some of his book-buying rounds as well. Not all of them, of course, but when I went out on my own, especially to the Montsweag Flea Market, I would discover that, no matter how early I got up, Frank would always have gotten there ahead of me and scooped up all the good books. It became quite frustrating for me.

One Saturday or Sunday morning during the summer I arrived at Montsweag to find that Frank was still there, but well ahead of me. So I dragged along in his wake, looking at the stuff he'd rejected. There's an old saying in the book trade: Not everyone can be an expert in everything. His specialties didn't include modern first editions in particular, and I was interested in those, of course. I stopped at a stall to look at a few books and discovered a first edition of *Jonathan Livingston Seagull* by Richard Bach that Frank had missed. It was in good condition with a dustjacket, so I bought it for a dollar or under and later sold it for a few hundred dollars. The best part of that deal, though, was knowing I had beaten Frank McQuaid at his own game that once, anyway.

Another person who roped me into the bookselling business was Charlie Davis, still a legendary character in Oswego, New York, and in the worlds of folklore and jazz as well. He turned from music to business to poetry and fiction writing and editing. He established his own publishing company, The Mathom Publishing Company, in 1977, two years before The Mathom Bookshop of Dresden, Maine, was founded.

For many years Davis had been a partner in a local business firm, Brown-Davis Furniture, and when he decided to return to college in the mid-1970s he was half-retired. Retirement for Charlie simply meant expanding his horizons — not that they had been previously very limited. One might say he now had more time to devote to his vocations. Two of these had always been music and verse composition. He began by taking a course in poetry writing with Roger Dickinson-Brown, then a member of the staff of my Program in Writing Arts at SUNY Oswego.

Davis had grown up in Indiana. His father had been a close friend of a neighbor, James Whitcomb Riley, the "Hoosier Poet," and Charlie early came under Riley's benevolent influence. Later on, Charlie graduated from Notre Dame University and, upon his graduation, organized a group of musicians during the hey-day of the Big Bands — he wrote about it in his book, published by Mathom, *That Band from Indiana* — and was very successful on the swing and hot jazz circuits. Those of you who watched Ken Burns' history of jazz on PBS may have noticed a marquee at the Brooklyn Theatre that read, "Charlie Davis and His Joy Gang," which shared the billing with a young singer named Ethel Merman. Charlie's band singer was another young person named Dick Powell. One of his compositions of the period was "Copenhagen," a jazz classic that has been performed by nearly all the famous swing and jazz artists since it was introduced. The composer drew royalties from it twice a year until his death in his nineties.

The first course Davis took was titled "The Nature of Poetry." It was a beginner's course, but stringent and technical. In it the student must write verse exercises in every prosody, schema, and genre imaginable.

Davis did well for Dickinson-Brown, and he began to involve himself in the extensive literary scene on campus. He gave readings with other students, and his work was always popular because it was . . . "quaint" is the only word to describe it. The Riley influence was clear, at least to the faculty if not to the students, who had never heard of the Hoosier Poet.

When Davis asked to take the second course in the sequence of three undergraduate poetry courses in the Program he was asked whether he had ever completed a BA. He replied that he had a PhB in business administration from Notre Dame, and he was denied permission to take the course, but he was told that he could enroll in the graduate seminar titled "Conference Course in Writing Poetry," which he did. I taught it. He was told that the project of the course involved writing a long poem, something he had never done, and he was (atypically for the class) given a proscription: he was not to write a single rhymed couplet. Instead, he was going to do something difficult. Difficult for him, that is.

"But what?" he asked, baffled.

"Well, have you ever heard of William Carlos Williams?"

"No, should I have?"

"Yes, since he's a famous contemporary of yours. Your first assignment is to read Williams' *Paterson.*"

Davis did so. No sooner had he digested the book than he began to write . . . *And So the Irish Built a Church,* a story about Oswego written, like *Paterson,* in prose and verse, with diary entries, newspaper clippings, songs, and what-have-you (it is impossible for the reader to identify what Davis invented and what he researched), tossed together in a seemingly random, but for all that, nevertheless, highly wrought mélange of lore and character and incident. Davis got so carried away that he even composed a pseudo-nineteenth century musical piece and copied it out on aged paper suitably charred to look as though it had been saved from the conflagration that had consumed the original church.

The other members of the class were no less busy than Charlie Davis, and as the semester developed it became obvious that this was a remarkable group of students doing fine things. The Davis piece was not the first work to be published from that class, but he was without doubt writing the longest work — it turned out to be 120 pages in length — and the most popular. Everyone was interested in reading the next installment though Charlie, doing something totally new and experimental for him (except where he managed to sneak in a rhymed song against orders), could not believe his classmates were not dissembling when they applauded him.

Since its publication in book form, there have been people who know W. C. Williams who claim that . . . *And So the Irish* . . . is more readable than its model. Since *Paterson* is a modern classic, this opinion is heretical. The main criticism of the Davis opus may be that it begins to a degree shakily. Riley is recognizable in the sentiment, and Williams in the form: the two do not mix well early on. But as the book progresses, Riley and Williams disappear and Davis rises above his sources to become one of the most engaging literary personalities of the late twentieth century, just as the man himself was larger than life.

Well, when Charlie had finished, he told me he was too old to start sending his book around to publishers and wait for them to accept it. He thought he would do it himself. So he gave himself, with my kibitzing, a short course in book publishing. When *The Irish* appeared it soon sold out, and Charlie decided to start his final career as a publisher. He asked me for a name for the press. I suggested "Mathom." He asked what that meant. I told him it was a word out of *The Hobbit* and *Lord of the Rings* that described the sort of things that filled the burrow homes of Bilbo and Frodo Baggins: things that one had no earthly use for, but that one simply couldn't bear to throw away. Charlie thought that accurately described the sorts of things he and I would publish (without asking, he assigned me as Editor-in-Chief of Mathom).

Two years later, in 1979, I established my summer project, the Mathom Bookshop of Dresden, Maine, which would be the major outlet for the books we published. In 1996 I retired from teaching and turned my attention full time (more or less) to the bookshop. Two of the last books Mathom published in Oswego were Charlie Davis' *The Lake Trout and Legend Society's Cookbook,* 1980, and the story of Charlie's career as a musical director, *That Band from Indiana,* 1982. One of the two latest is my book of poetry *The Green Maces of Autumn, Voices in an Old Maine House,* which was issued in 2002. It is a series of monologues by the people who live in the 1754 house built by Sylvester Gardiner on the property where my wife's family has lived for a century or two, and where the

Mathom Bookshop was located in the barn.

However, I opened my shop in the tractor garage of the farm on Blinn Hill Road and began to sell some of the books I'd accumulated. I started out with one short shelf of books, and I put a handmade sign out on the road. Pretty soon I added a shelf, and then another and another, and then I was building permanent bookshelves. One day the Maine State DOT stopped by to tell me I needed to register my business with the sales tax office, and my signs had to conform to rules and regulations. Things were beginning to get expensive.

While I was in the garage I sold my books cheaply. Customers would stop by, and when they'd bought what they wanted they'd tell my wife that I was charging too little for my collection. In 1995 I decided to salvage the barn. I put a new floor into the northwest corner where it had collapsed, then built a room on it with shelves, lighting, a phone and other amenities. The next thing I had to do was move my books from the garage into the new bookshop, and while I was doing that, I decided to clean out my junk books and re-price everything.

One of the books I ran across while I was doing this was a beat-up loose-leaf black cloth notebook bound in half red leather and holding a set of printed pamphlets, 390 pages in all, constituting a course in *Business Law* taught at M.I.T. during the school year 1895–96. The pamphlets were in very good shape, but the binder was well worn and the spine was crumbling. It belonged to "C. B. Paine," who apparently took the course during his "2nd year," according to an ink notation on the rear pastedown. In the garage I'd had a sticker price on this item of ten cents.

There were two semesters' worth of printed pamphlets in the binder, held in upside down by short cords. The name of the teacher was on none of the first semester pamphlets, but on those of the second semester I found the name of the instructor: Louis D. Brandeis, later to become Justice of the United States Supreme Court. His specialty was business law, and, indeed, he was teaching at MIT in the pertinent years.

Obviously, I was no longer going to sell the binder and its contents for ten cents! But what price was I going to put on it? 1995 was the year when the Mathom Bookshop went on line, so I warmed up the computer, looked in Bookfinder.com and everywhere else I could think of, but could find no trace of another copy anywhere in the world. All I could do was shrug my shoulders and put an arbitrary price on the Brandeis item. I thought $800.00 sounded pretty good. As soon as *Business Law* appeared on line a Washington attorney snapped it up. I suspect I could have gotten a bit more than $800.00 for it, but at least my second price was better than my first!

It was never hard to find books to sell. In fact, they found me. People were always calling me up to ask if I bought books, and of course I bought many more books than I sold, so my stock increased exponentially. One day, after I'd moved from the garage into the renovated barn, I arrived there to discover one of my neighbors had left piles of boxes filled with her collection of cookbooks in front of the barn door. I was fortunate that it hadn't rained. She didn't want payment, she just wanted to get rid of her books.

Another day during the winter I received a phone call from a young man in Richmond who said he had a jeepful of books to sell. I went over to look at them. It was a pretty ordinary lot. I said I'd buy them for two hundred dollars if he'd deliver them to the bookshop. He agreed.

It took me weeks to go through the books, decide which ones I'd donate to the Dresden Library book sale, as I did every year, and which ones I'd keep and catalog. One of the first books I looked at, a large tabletop production, annoyed me greatly. The author was someone named Slim Aarons, and it was titled *A Wonderful Time: An Intimate Portrait of the Good Life,* published in 1974. It was all about how great it was to be rich in those times. The volume was in very good shape with a dust jacket, but it so offended me that I threw it up on top of an old appliance standing there in the barn and left it for last.

Finally, when I had finished dealing with all the other books, I looked up the Aarons book on the web to see if it was listed and what it was worth. I found that, indeed, it was listed, and that I had by far the best copy of it in the world. My copy was perfect with a perfect dust jacket; all others had some flaw or imperfection. And each of the available copies, of which there were few, was worth hundreds of dollars. I was amazed. Why would anybody want to buy such an idiotic book? However, no sooner had I put it into my on-line catalogue than a rare books dealer in New York City bought it for what was apparently my favorite price to charge, $800.00. If a dealer was willing to pay that much for it, imagine what he was going to sell it for, because dealers usually buy a book for between a quarter and a third of its retail value, unless they can get it for less.

By the way, I have recently finished reading a book by one of my favorite authors, Umberto Eco. Titled *The Mysterious Flame of Queen Loana,* it is about an Italian rare books dealer who has had a stroke and, when he comes out of it, he remembers nothing of his actual life, only the books he has read over the years since he was a child. I recommend it to anyone at all interested in books: comic books, dime novels, collecting books, World War II … in fact, I simply recommend it to anyone who loves reading a good book.

All my life I have enjoyed collecting and reading books, and selling them, too, but I was making no real profit from my retirement business despite the occasional windfall. In fact, my rising overhead was getting to the point where I could hardly break even anymore, so the Mathom Bookshop closed its doors officially on the last day of December, 2006. I began selling off some of my stock, mostly duplicates, in small auctions, but the first auction of some of my really good remaining books took place at the Thomaston Place Auction Galleries of Thomaston, Maine, and on-line on Saturday, June 30th, 2007.

It was a beautiful early summer day. The sun was bright, Route One was beginning to fill up with traffic, but when we pulled into the parking lot of the auction house we saw very few cars. "I was afraid of this," I told Jean. "Who's going to attend an auction on a day like this one?"

Inside I thought I'd see some fellow members of the Maine Antiquarian Booksellers Association, but I recognized no one. That was alarming. Then I saw in the catalogue that most of the books in the auction were books on architecture, and those were the ones the people present were after. Sure enough, some of my best books went for pennies on the dollar while others weren't bid on at all. "Not a very literary crowd, I guess, eh?" I said to one of the auctioneers on my way out to join Jean in the car where she had earlier retreated to avoid the depressing sale.

FAILED FATHERS

On a theme by, and with apologies to, Greg Pape.

By January of 1955, when my ship, the aircraft carrier *USS Hornet* (CVA12), pulled into San Diego and I was reunited with my Buffalo babysitter, Cousin Josie, she had already been married and divorced twice. She was then (and ever after) a single mother. Since she was only eleven years or so older than I was and a Navy veteran of the Second World War to boot, she had clearly been pretty busy since the last time I'd seen her.

Josie told me that the first of her two husbands had been a lush, and the second had been a mama's boy. I don't remember the name of number one, if I ever knew it, but number two was Higgins, and he gave his monicker to his little daughter, Georgette.

I never met either of Josie's husbands, and I know nothing of what happened to them subsequent to their divorces. Georgette — "Gigi," that is — has never spoken to me about her father, and every now and then I wonder what became of him.

Where do all the failed fathers
go? To Albuquerque? Cleveland?
After the slow slide down the drain,
where do they go? After the last
lay-off, the class reunion where they're shown

kissing the matronly Queen
of the Prom, where do they go. Where
do they go, these old young men, these
paunchy guys with the eyes that squint
into the lens at the family picnic,

the fishing expedition
near the falls, the baseball game where
they played second? After the fights,
the money fights, the brief affair,
after the spree and the morning after,

where *do* the failed fathers go?

Is there a bar where they gather,
is there a bus they all take,
is there a line at the Bureau
where they talk over their sons and daughters,

their Old Ladies turning cold,
the postmen they caught spending time
drinking coffee in their kitchens?
Is there a motel in Cleveland
full of fathers playing poker,

smoking cigarettes, squinting
at their hands, drinking beer? Is there,
down in Albuquerque, some street
full of walk-up rooms full of dreams
of mowing lawns, of paneling basements,

propping children on their bikes,
walking down the aisles of markets
pushing shopping carts? Of course, we
know what happens to our mothers,
but where oh where do the failed fathers go?

"LITTLE" JOSEPHINE

Except for their father and mother, the Sardellas were a family of teachers, even Josephine, the younger sister, who began as a Navy nurse in World War II and continued her career afterward until she quit and got a job teaching health in the Buffalo public schools for twenty years. Joseph, the eldest sibling, taught engineering in a junior college in California; Salvatore, the younger brother, taught shop in Buffalo, and Sarah, the older sister, was a grade school teacher in the Buffalo suburb of North Tonawanda, as was her second husband, Bernard Moretti.

There had originally been seven Sardella cousins, three of whom I never knew. The first was Luigi, named after my father who arrived in the U. S. in 1914 with his older sister Vita Sardella to find her husband, Salvatore Sardella, Sr., who was then living in Wakefield, Massachusetts. He had left his family in Riesi, Sicily, telling his wife he would send for her once he was established in the New World. Vita eventually had gotten tired of waiting, so she had opened a shoe shop to earn enough money to come over with her children. My father worked in the shop also, and he came with her. He was twenty-four years old when they arrived.

The baby Luigi was born a year later with a defective colon that killed him in 1918, even though he had undergone a pioneering colostomy. Angelo the First was born next, in 1916; he died of the flu during the epidemic of 1919, not long before the next baby was born, Angelo the Second, who lasted fourteen years, until 1933 — the year before I was born — burning to death in an accident: he had been building a raft out of oil drums on which he had been using a blowtorch. Next came Joseph, Salvatore, Jr., Sarah, and Josephine. By this time Vita and her children had left the father and moved with my dad to Buffalo.

I had been born in Buffalo and lived near my cousins the first four years of my life. "Little" Josie, fourteen when I was born, had been my baby sitter. Later, she was a Navy nurse during World War II, and she had wound up in San Diego, not far from her older brother and his family who lived in La Mesa. As a young adult I got to know Josie again while I was myself serving four years in the Navy, for in January of 1955 my ship, the *USS Hornet,* was in San Diego, and I would sometimes go to spend the weekend with my cousin Joseph, his wife "Big" Josephine (my mother's closest friend in the family) and their children, Virginia and Eddie, in La Mesa. I remember that Ginger (no one ever called her Virginia) had to walk around in a body cast because she had a terrible case of scoliosis. In hot weather that cast must have been unbearable.

At Joe's I spent a lot of time playing ping-pong at which he always won. I wasn't keen on frustration, so I spent most of my liberties with my other cousins, so-called "Little" Josephine — to distinguish her from Joe's wife — and her daughter Gigi (Georgette, but nobody ever called her that), who lived in the city itself. I remember we went to the zoo, and to the ballet to see Maria Tallchief dance, and once I brought some of my buddies from the ship over for a spaghetti dinner, but mostly we talked.

In San Diego I heard a lot of family lore involving Josie's mother, my Aunty Vita, a long-suffering woman whom I recall vividly, though I saw her seldom after my family had moved from Buffalo to Meriden, Connecticut. I was amazed to realize, when Josie told me in February, 2000, that I had been only seven when she died, for I still feel a great affection for her. Josie says it was reciprocated, and that's what I remember too, despite the fact that I was such a hellion, apparently. The most famous example of my infernal nature had to do with a new Easter outfit my mother bought me when I was two years old. It's a story Josie loved to tell, and did so every time we got together.

There were three pieces to the little suit: a pair of shorts, a jacket, and a cap, all in a checked fabric I remember from a photo portrait, perhaps the occasion for which the outfit was purchased. According to Josie my father was furious with my mother for buying it because it was expensive and we were in the throes of the Great Depression — we really couldn't afford it. But the cost of the suit turned out to be the smallest part of the expenditure because when I heard my parents arguing about the outfit, Josie said, I evidently assumed that getting rid of the offending items would settle the contretemps, so I flushed the cap down Aunty Vita's toilet. That plugged the sewer line, and the city had to come out and dig up the street to get rid of the obstruction. Evidently my parents never understood why I had done what I had done, but Josie knew.

From 1965 I taught at the State University of New York College at Oswego, not terribly far down the New York Thruway from Buffalo, and there had been visits back and forth between the first and second generations of cousins on various occasions, in particular Thanksgivings, but it wasn't until Eastertide of nineteen-ninety-three that all the remaining Buffalo cousins came to Oswego for dinner.

Josie, whose idea it was, came with Gigi. Bernie and Sarah Sardella Moretti, Josie's childless sister, came also, and Linda Sardella Boucher came up from New

London with her third husband, Ray. Everyone stayed overnight, but Linda and Ray had to use a motel as there wasn't enough room in the house, what with my wife, Jean, and me, and our daughter, Melora, taking up two of the three bedrooms.

Linda is my late favorite cousin Salvatore's daughter, raised by "Little" Josie after Sal, a widower, died on a couch in the living room while watching TV. According to Josie, her surrogate motherhood of Linda had been "arranged" by Joe, his wife "Big" Josie, my mother and my father who all thought it was a great idea which would inconvenience no one — if one discounted Little Josie who hadn't married a third time. She was persuaded to move from San Diego back to Buffalo into the home that Sal had owned. She had not been happy about being manipulated in such a manner, and she evidently never let Linda forget it. Linda returned the favor and left as soon as she could to attend Ithaca College, not far from Oswego. She met John Greven there.

Linda's first husband was a boy, really, when they came to visit us in Oswego for Christmas one year. They brought their new baby, Jessica, but *all* of them were young and the marriage didn't last. Linda had subsequently led an unhappy life for twenty-five years or so.

One year Jessica too had come to visit us in Oswego, but despite the upheavals of her early life she seemed to be as well-adjusted as anyone might wish. She became a forest ranger in Canton, New York — I don't know why she didn't come down for Easter with the rest of the cousins, but then my son, Christopher, was elsewhere also.

Linda's third husband Ray Boucher was older. Jean and I had attended their wedding in Connecticut on September 25th of 1990, the last time almost all the cousins had been together. The wedding was a big church affair, unlike her two other ventures into matrimony, and everyone had a grand time. Even Ginger Sardella Lloyd came east from California; her younger brother Ed was the only one not to make it. This was the first time my wife Jean and I had met Ginger's husband, Farquhar Telynin Lloyd III, a Welshman wisely known to all as "Jim." Ginger lived not far from her widowed mother Big Josie, who survived until 2004.

Little Josie brought the entire 1993 Easter dinner: a lamb roast with all the accessories and trimmings. She wouldn't let Sarah into the kitchen, but Jean, Melora, and Gigi helped while Linda and I sat talking. On Josie's suggestion, Jean had bought a big cake to celebrate Bernie's birthday, which had occurred earlier in the week. This was the first time I'd spent any time at all with Bernie, or — since I was a little kid living in Buffalo myself — with Sarah.

About that birthday party: it was the final skirmish in the eternal sibling feud between Little Josie and Sarah, though Bernie was delighted. Josie pulled it as a surprise, not only on him, but on her sister as well, and Sarah wasn't pleased, one could clearly tell — Gigi kept running back and forth between her mother and her aunt trying to keep the peace. I'm sure Sarah would not have driven down for Easter if she had had an inkling. On the other hand, Josie, who had never had a good word to say about Bernie, was as smug as a cat purring over her coup. Bernie kept saying that he and Sarah were going to invite us all up to Buffalo soon for another gathering, but that never happened. Instead, he and Sarah disappeared — our 1996 and '97 Christmas cards came back marked "addressee unknown" — and it wasn't until 1998 that I heard, belatedly through Little Josie, that her sister and Bernie had moved out to Las Vegas, Nevada, where she had died of cancer on the 27th of January, 1998. Sarah had not told Little Josie or Gigi that she was leaving, or even that she was ill, and neither she nor Bernie ever sent their address or phone number to any of us. Josie says that whenever she and Gigi talk about Sarah they do so weeping.

In 1996 I retired from teaching at S.U.N.Y. Oswego and we moved to Maine, though Jean and I kept our home in upstate New York. We return periodically, especially in the spring during black fly season in Maine: I am deathly allergic to their bites. Nevertheless, Jean and I have spent summers and most of our leisure time there since the year before our marriage, 1955. Both her mother and father were born and raised in Dresden, Maine.

The house in Dresden Mills is called the Cate Farm, Cate being another of my wife's family names and her middle name as well. On the property there is a barn in which I had a summer store, The Mathom Bookshop, from 1979 to 2007. In 1996 the shop became my "full time" project, and a couple of years later it went on the internet where it really did become almost full time.

Jean and I moved to Dresden Mills partly because our daughter was a librarian in nearby Winthrop. Another reason for our remove to Maine, though, was because both my mother-in-law Bertha Getchell Houdlette and Jean's eldest sister, Nathalie Ahern, were very ill. Jean's mother died the same year, 1996, at the age of 96, but Nathalie lingered on for six years, until 2002, so she was alive for the second Turco family reunion of cousins, held in Dresden Mills on June 22nd, 2001.

There was a large contingent present from various localities in Connecticut including my brother, Gene; his wife, Judy; their two sons, Scott and Stephen, with his wife Christine and their toddler son Jack (!). Scott brought not only his fiancée,

Shannon, but her twin sister, Kourtney, Irish-American lasses. Linda and Ray Boucher came up from Quaker Hill, but Jessica, who is married now, didn't make it.

Gigi had decided she couldn't come, so Josie, at age 81 and ill, drove herself from Buffalo to Linda's house in Quaker Hill, Connecticut, and the Bouchers drove her from there to Dresden Mills. Jean and I were amazed, but she showed up little the worse for wear.

Linda told me that Ginger Lloyd would have liked to be invited. I was sorry not to have asked her, but when we were considering invitations we decided that California was probably too far to ask anyone to come from. Christopher, a professional musician, came from Silver Spring, Maryland, on the way through New York City, there picking up a family friend from Oswego, Kate Auleta, and of course Melora and Jessima came over from Lewiston, Maine, where they were living at the time.

The weather was hot. Nathalie was quite ill, so the festivities weren't held at the Cate Farm but up the road a little way where Jean and I live in a home owned by her sister Betty Falton and rented to us. We treated everyone to lobsters out on the front lawn under a couple of canopies I managed to put up, though portions collapsed from time to time. My young nephews kept propping them up.

Little Josie hadn't spent much time with my brother and his family, because he was born and raised entirely outside of Buffalo. Since the various cousins hadn't spent a great deal of time together, the reunion was a good way to get acquainted and for Linda to choose to make peace with her aunt, which she did. This wasn't the first time that Linda had been in Dresden Mills. As a teen-ager she had spent a summer with us at the farm. She and Jean's nephew Peter, Nathalie's son, had spent some of their sunny days picking big red raspberries in the patch out back of the house and selling them in a stand they set up out in front, under the huge old elm that used to shade the dooryard.

While the Dresden Mills reunion was going on I led an expedition down into our back yard where there is a brook and a little waterfall, a millrace, really, where the foundations of a shingle mill remain. We walked down to the Cate farm and looked at the foundations and grindstones of another of the structures that give our section of Dresden its name, a gristmill. We went in to visit Jean's fading sister, and then we went out to look through my bookshop in the barn.

The reunion was a complete success, but the thing I remember best about the affair is that Josephine, sitting in our kitchen at one point, looked up and was amazed to see hummingbirds at our feeder in the window. She was utterly delighted — she had never seen hummingbirds before!

Jean and I hosted another reunion in Dresden on 17 September of 2005. Josie didn't come because she had been hospitalized with complications from her diabetes, and Gigi stayed with her in Buffalo, but Jim & Ginger Lloyd came from California; Linda came with her friend from Connecticut, as did my brother Gene and his wife Judy, but their sons with their families couldn't make it. Ed and Sandy Sardella came from Colorado, Jessica Craycroft, Linda's daughter, came from Utah, Chris came from Woodstock, New York, and Melora, with her daughter, Jessima, and her husband Steve Norman with his daughters — Siri, by his first wife, and Phoebe, our younger granddaughter — all attended.

Although it rained so much that Chris and I had to put plastic sheeting up on the screens of the front porch where I'd set up tables, we all were dry as we ate our dinner catered by Mark Antony's Italian restaurant in Wiscasset. There was supposed to be food enough for twenty, but in fact there was enough for forty. We had a grand time despite the dismal weather.

Because Josie and Gigi had missed the reunion, the following November, just before Thanksgiving, Jean and I drove up to Buffalo to see them. This time it was we who brought food, from Canale's Restaurant in Oswego. Gigi provided some excellent condiments at Josie's behest. Although we didn't know it, when we said goodbye that day to drive back to Oswego, it was the last time we would see Little Josephine: on the 12th of August 2006 Gigi called to tell us that her mother was dead. Her memorial service would be held on the 19th.

On Wednesday the 22nd Jean and I left Dresden, spent Thursday in Oswego, drove to Buffalo on Friday where we stayed in Josie's apartment overnight and went to the memorial service at a funeral home incredibly named "Amigone." Aside from the tacky name, the whole performance was tasteful although the hired preacher was a former bouncer — well over six feet — and faculty member at SUNY Canton who didn't fake anything. I had prepared a little memoir of Josie and the cousins, most of whom were present: Gigi, Linda and her escort, Ginger and Jim Lloyd. Gene and Judy couldn't come because they had a family wedding the same day, and Eddie was doing something in the service of his wife. The only surprise was that I was pressed into service as the solo pallbearer.

At the gravesite (where Linda's parents Salvatore and Margine are also buried) I carried her ashes in a porcelain casque. There was a marine honor guard with a live bugler to play Taps. Afterward we went to Gigi's house for refreshments, and shortly thereafter Jean and I left for Oswego and, eventually, Dresden.

POCOANGELINI

A Review by Felix Stefanile

The gallery of portraits, of characters, is a traditional poetic mode of ancient lineage. Mr. Turco has given us his contributions to this form in other books. His *Pocoangelini: A Fantography and Other Poems* (1973) contains three sequences: "Pocoangelini," "The Sketches" [1962], and "Bordello." The "Pocoangelini" sequence, not related in theme to the other two sections, runs sixty-four pages. "Bordello," a mere ten. The three parts joined together in this way, unrelated as they are, give the book a jerry-built feeling, and my impression is that the superior poems in the collection deserved better editing. "Bordello" struck me as nothing new, a series of ballad-like pieces dealing with men and women and sex, all perhaps a little too prettily, too literarily stated.

"Pocoangelini" describes the spiritual journeying of a Quixote-like, Ariel-like, Adam-like character who undergoes a series of changes in a strange, dark, yet glittering world. Turco is a metrically skillful poet, and the Adam paradigm fits:

POCOANGELINI 12

She is caught in her frail house
as Poco is caught in his. The rib she stole
is the furniture of his breast. Poco puts
his ear to listen to the nameless Word
her lung suspires into blood, and the word
redounds, echoes out of the breath
of his own mouth.
                                        Listen. She would have
seed of Pocoangelini. She would bring
more bone forth to walk among the walkers,
to chisel rimes upon monuments
in the fields among groves and grass —
the boudoir where lovers lie at last.

Elsewhere Pocoangelini has conversations with a mouse, with Mr. Earth, the moon, the mirror, a dandelion, and encounters magical situations.

Turco seems to have the whole of the English lyric tradition at his fingertips, and though this is not entirely a good thing — too much tinkle here and there, here a bit of Keats, there a bit of Mother Goose — I belong to the old school and see in this bravura the commitment of a poet to craft. I trust poets who show clear influences, and I don't trust the groggy, toneless, "spontaneous" mutter of much that goes by the name of verse today among the younger, studiously untutored poets of the Confessional school. Many of the poems of the "Pocoangelini" sequence were first published in magazines like *Tri-Quarterly, Saturday Review,* and *Poetry.*

I would like to see Turco, who is an actively publishing poet as well as teacher — his *Poetry: An Introduction through Writing* is one of the more original poetry texts on the market — return to the inspiration of "The Sketches," the sequence that forms the middle third of this book. There, in a handful of character vignettes — A. R. Ammons called them "an autobiography of biographies" — we have a poet who is direct, clear-seeing, musical, and quite real. Poems like "Guido the Ice-House Man," "Ercole the Butcher," and "Mrs. Martino the Candy Store Lady" speak to the human condition with grace, always a strong point with Turco, and warmth. Just as important, I think the resistance of the subject matter — real people, often simple, not particularly highly endowed — works well with this poet's tendency to treat his material with too much "fanciness." A tension is set up between the nubbiness of the material and the neatness of Turco's technique:

Listen to the hum
    of the lemon ice machine, mashing
    sugar, mushing ice, crushing
    the puckerbellies of chubby lemons.
"Twenty minutes, can you wait?
    Twenty minutes for lemon ice,"
    mumbles Mrs. Martino.
"Meanwhile, have a Milky Way;
    look, they've been in the Frigidaire;
    they're hard as bricks, they'll
    freeze your teeth —
    look, have a Milky Way."
So nibble while the engine jiggles,
    the ice goes smash, the candy bars
    go limp behind your teeth
    and twenty minutes spin around;

twenty minutes spin around.

There are shadows in the shop;
there are candies on the counter;
there is ice cream in the freezer —
but your eyes are on the accordion cups
the lemon ice is eaten from

And twenty minutes is like sluggish ice
as the cups grow larger with your eyes.

Precision of language, and to be envied.

A LETTER TO MY COUSIN

by Ann Buttigheri Badach

Westwood, New Jersey
25 January 2007

Dear Lew,

The book of recollections you sent me, *Shaking the Family Tree,* now brings together in my mind my stepmother's stories about "The Sardellas of Buffalo." My own and my sister Catina's birth mother died in 1935. Our father, Salvatore Buttigheri, heard through our family grapevine that there was a lovely woman in the hometown that my dad and yours came from — Riesi, Sicily, of course — and he should go back to check her out. He did, and the rest is history.

My father was thirteen years older than your cousin Fina — Filomena Dierna — who was twenty-three years old at the time. I called her "Mom" because I never knew my birth mother who died one month after I was born. My sister Catina ("Tina") was almost four. Mom was the daughter of your father's and Vita's younger sister Beatrice.

My Mom's admiration for their older sister, your Aunt Vita, was unquestionable. I remember Vita visiting us in Jersey City during my very early years — soon after mom came to this country. Vita brought Mom a patchwork quilt (so Americanish, if that's a word) that I can still remember: it was a collage of pink fabrics, and it was on my mother's bed for many, many years.

Vita taught my mother how to make "American Apple Pie" and "American Donuts" and gave her any number of "American Recipes." I'm using quotes because that's the way Mom entitled them in her handwritten recipe book. How modern of Vita to assimilate so quickly. She must have learned them from your Yankee mother while the Turco and Sardella families were living together in Buffalo. Vita remains in my mind as a little woman with a slight dowager's hump, a perky hat and sensible shoes. As a kid I thought she didn't smile too much, but what did I know of her hardships?

I enjoyed so much your memoir of your cousin and Vita's daughter, "Little Josephine," the ex-Navy nurse of World War II who died last year, in 2006. I remember she came to visit when I was a very young child and in awe of her uniform. The shiny gold buttons and gold insignia on her cap, the cape with the red satin lining and her presence, which loomed so large and important. How differently life is perceived by the eye of the child.

To her credit, although she apparently suffered many physical and emotional problems, Vita also gave Mom the courage she needed to get through the dark days that were to come. Appropriate, isn't it? "Vita" means "life," and it was she who gave my mother the life-sustaining support she so desperately needed. These two Sicilian women were brave, tenacious, uncomplaining and strong — although my mother eventually broke down one day years later and told me of her early depression.

In only her early twenties, she was far from her family — in those days Europe was a million light years away from Jersey City. She had great difficulty learning the English language, was married into a hostile family environment, had to care for a cantankerous and creepy old man (my grandfather Buttigheri), and be mother to two small children. Poor Tina would cry for our natural mother night after night. In those days — the early 40's, during the war — letters from Europe came through the Red Cross. We would have to travel a long distance by bus to go to the Red Cross station to pick up an infrequent but treasured letter from Mom's family.

The worst part of these early years was that there was no escape. For Mom to return to Italy was not even remotely possible. Divorce? Disgrace. Shame. Immaturity. Fortunately, she and my Aunt Louise, my dad's brother's wife, were the same age and Louise too had to put up with the "hostile family" of Buttigheris. They shared many hardships and were a great comfort to each other. Aunt Louise is still (2007) with us. She lives at an assisted living complex and will soon be 94. She is the last of my mother's generation here in the U.S.

I believe that the generation of "the Depression" was one of America's strongest, and I believe that the word "depression" took on more meaning than the crash and burning of the American economy. I never once heard my father or mother complain that there wasn't enough money or show signs of despondency. My father worked at the barbershop from 6:30 a.m. to 7:00 p.m. giving haircuts for 15 cents and shaves for 10 cents during the '30s and '40s, and my mother was a homemaker who became a magician by turning one penny into two. Both of our parents worked extremely hard. My sister and I were certainly not raised in the lap of luxury, but I don't remember ever wanting for something — maybe I just didn't know any better.

There was one thing I always wanted, though — a bike, but Mom saw to it that I didn't have one because I might get hurt or be killed and then the blame for that would rest on her shoulders and she would be judged as an "unfit stepmother." If anything tragic were to happen to either of us children it would be grist for the Sicilian family gossip mill both here and in Italy for years to come, most especially for the Cassaros, my natural mother's family. So, because of her need to "prove herself a fit mother" I stayed with safe and cultural pastimes, one of which was that my father insisted Tina and I take piano lessons. We did that for six years. Neither of us made it to Carnegie Hall.

Despite the Depression, the cold water flat we lived in and the proverbial hand-me-downs, we always had a car, notwithstanding that it was always about ten years old and rattled and clattered as we traveled. There was a Ford Model T in which, my mother said, we visited your father Zio Luigi and his family in Connecticut when I was very little, and every several feet it would backfire and spew sparks and smoke. But we continued on our trip, safely reaching our destination, and then back home again — quite a feat for both that poor excuse for a car and my dad the driver, considering it was from Jersey City to Meriden, more than 100 miles.

When I think back on the times when it was your dad who would come to visit us, they were hilarious. He would enter through our front door and my dad would respectfully greet him, then turn around and go out the back door because he knew it would take no more than ten minutes into the visit before your dad, so zealous in his Protestant faith, would begin to evangelize. It wasn't that my dad was Roman Catholic, but that he was not religious. At the time, Catholics still observed the "no meat on Friday" ruling. If my dad would not observe the "fish only" meal, he would say that it was a sin what came out of one's mouth and not what went in. On looking back at his rationalization and the Church's subsequent discontinuance of that stupid church law, I have to say that he was certainly ahead of his time.

Even I, at such a young age, would challenge your dad and throw some of the observances of the Catholic faith at him, insisting that they were dogma and it was the one and only true faith (that's how Rome brainwashed us). He would simply smile and say that I didn't understand what faith was really all about. It would infuriate me, but in retrospect, he too was way ahead of his time. If only Rome would learn to simplify! Yes, of course, I'm still a practicing Catholic, though with a mind of my own, but I have to say that your dad certainly gave cause for one to stop and think, and think and think. He would have made a great Protestant "Pope." We could have called him "Pope Luigi the First." Viva Il Pape!

My apologies for not addressing the question of the invisible Italian

Protestants. Your essay, "The Story of an Italian Protestant" is so very, very interesting. Your research boggles my mind. You write that Italy is predominately Catholic; yes, I agree it was and is still, but ever so fragilely. However, my mom told me that there were many Protestants in Riesi. Mom's sister Sarina and her husband, Gaetano Naso, were dyed-in-the-wool Protestants as were many members of their family, thanks to your dad's influence.

The irony here is that my mother's brother Felice became a Catholic priest, and when Zio Luigi went to Italy and found out that Felice had entered the seminary, he was very upset. He would harangue his sister Beatrice and ask how she could let such a thing happen. The story goes that times were very tough, so Felice was sent away to a not-so-nearby town to learn a trade. He took room and board at the local Catholic seminary while he was being trained. A priest who was a resident of the seminary and who had a very convincing argument for "the calling" approached Felice and recognized that he was a perfect candidate for the priesthood. He saw that Felice had a strong character, that he was diligent in his work, kind, and a very good student. Perfect!

Your dad never quite got over it, but I'm told that in the end they both recognized that it was their faith that was paramount and not which church they attended. Your dad was so motivated and so zealous. I still have a bible he sent to me dated 1947; the pages have turned brown, but on the inside cover there is a presentation plate which he inscribed, "To Anna Buttigheri with the wishes of the blessing of God, as a Christmas gift, 1947," and he signed it, "Your uncle, Luigi Turco." I must regretfully admit it is not worn from usage. What great faith he had even in light of his early struggles. Thank you for sharing his story with me. I shall read it again and again.

Though my own father was not a religious man, he was the eternal optimist. My mother was the wary one. More times than not, it was my father's optimism that got us through the hard times. Eventually, through really hard work, frugality, a bit of tenacity and courage, prosperity finally came about and our cars got bigger and better, we got the requisite T.V. in a mahogany cabinet, and my father, without telling my mother, had a baby grand piano delivered to our home. She thought the deliverymen were nuts. But sure enough, it was ours.

Well, I didn't expect to run on so, but you've awakened so many memories which have lain dormant in the dusty corners of my mind for many, many years. Lew, it seems you relish this research of both your immediate and extended family. I recently saw the movie adaptation of Mitch Alborn's book *The Five People*

You Meet In Heaven, about a man who dies thinking his life had no significance, but at death he meets five people in whose lives, unbeknownst to him, he had played a major part. They show him that his life did have worth. There was a line in that movie that struck a chord with me: “we are all connected.” As I’m traveling along with you on this journey of discovery, I have to believe that it’s true.

Ciao, cugino,

Ann

P. S. One more thing: I’m quite sure it was your dad’s mother, Rosaria Fasulo Turco, who owned a grocery store downstairs from their living quarters in Riesi. Talk about a workaholic! Mom said that she worked that place 24/7 from sunrise to sunset. It was not a busy place, just an occasional customer: she sold pasta “loosely” — you know, grab a handful and wrap it in paper. As she got much older she adamantly refused to close shop. She would open up and sit there all day. She would exclaim, “What will I do without my store?” It gave her purpose and kept her connected to the community. She might even have died there, for all I know. She, too, was one tough cookie, not a “Hallmark” grandma.

STREET MEETING

A discussion by Stanley Romaine Hopper

Professor Rudolph Årnheim, in an extremely useful and cogent essay entitled, "Psychological Notes on the Poetical Process [from *Poets at Work,* essays based on the modern poetry collection at the Lockwood Memorial Library, University of Buffalo, by Rudolph Arnheim, W. H. Auden, Karl Shapiro, and Donald Stauffer, with an Introduction by Charles D. Abbott, New York: Harcourt, Brace, 1948], makes a number of highly relevant observations. I should like to note two or three of these.

There is, first of all, the movement from the "practical" (what we have called . . . the concrete or raw data of the poem's content) to the "poetical" — a necessary shift from "objective correctness" to a "subjective truth" which is essential to the poetic experience. This desirable and decisive shift he illustrates from the worksheets of a poem by Stephen Spender. The "practical" starting point of the poem is apparent in its first version:

> What is the use now of meeting and speaking:
> Always when we meet I think of another meeting
> Always when we speak I think of another speaking….

As the work on the poem progresses this version is made over into the following:

> Oh what is the use now of our meeting and speaking
> Since every meeting is thinking of another meeting
> Since all my speaking is groping for another speaking.

In the first version the practical facts of physical meeting and speaking on the one hand, and the psychological reflections arising from the meeting on the other, are stressed: while what is poetically significant is not disclosed. Also the persons involved are foremost, by way of the pronouns *we* and *I.* But in the second version the two kinds of happening — the physical and the psychological — are fused: what is poetically crucial is that which is contained in the paradox, or in the point of overlap, or identity, between the two contradictory happenings. By subordinating the persons to the deeper meaning of the events, and by fusing the contradictory elements in the language of the second form, the "poetical" meaning of the encounter is made to emerge. The time relationships of the first version are transformed into the following equation:

meeting = thinking of another meeting
speaking = groping for another speaking.

In the poem entitled "Street Meeting," by [Lewis] Turco, we see the same struggle taking place between the physical event of meeting, with its "practical" data, and the psychological effects of this meeting in the mind of the poet:

I saw him on the street.
His flesh was heavy.
For years we had not met:
Time takes its levy,
Returning ounce for hour.
But the eyes I'd known
Had stayed the same though flesh constricted bone.

His eyes owned all the past —
I saw it staring,
Bewildered, not at rest,
Still full of daring,
But fettered now by the hoar
Of revolving clocks:
A hurt, unlikely witch within its stocks.

I watched the troubled look
His face reflected
And knew he'd pick my lock
Had time defected.
But each of us could hear
Wary sentries call
And answer in the long, resounding hall.

We spoke in platitudes,
Each of us helpless,
The victims of our moods
And of our losses:

The present was the heir
Of our common past.
The future would inherit all at last.

Here the poet does not attempt so immediate and summary a fusion between the two. He shuttles from the one to the other throughout the first four stanzas, expanding and increasing the detail of each part, and retaining the dramatic presence of the persons. But this means that the paradox must reach its fusion in the concluding stanza, and must, as in a drama, effect a reconciliation of the opposites. Fortunately, the concluding stanza is the best in the poem, and the concluding line achieves *both* the paradox *and* the dramatic reconciliation:

We parted. Each of us
Had fanned an ember.
We'd shared another loss
And would remember.
But time was still for hire:
He walked off alone.
When next we meet our prisons will have grown.

This denouement is satisfactory (it satisfies). The emotion which the elements in conflict have set ajar are purged. The particulars are transcended and the "poetic" or subjective significance of the event comes clear.

REUNIONS

In 2002 Jean and I attended the 50th Anniversary Reunion of the Meriden High School Class of 1952. We drove our minivan down to Meriden on Friday, the 16th of August, through the hottest weather of the summer and terrible traffic with jams all the way down. But we made it to the Ramada just off East Main Street.

Our classmate and friend, Marie Delemarre Ho, still lived down a little way in her old family home, so Jean and I drove there with another classmate, Marie Schoneck, who was staying across the hall from us at the Ramada, to pick up the Dutch composer Walter Hekster (my collaborator on a chamber opera among other settings) and his wife, Alice Van Leuvan (a bassoonist, also our classmate), and drive them to the preliminary pizza party at the Hibernians' lodge in Tracy, near where I used to buy fireworks when I was a kid on a bicycle.

Jim Masterson was working away with Sheila, the wife of Chuck Verba, the bass in our old Sportlanders Quartet: he and I and Bill Niemec, a baritone, sang a few of the old songs. We did a couple of them okay *sans* tenor. Tomie DePaola, the children's writer and illustrator, was wandering around the room chatting with various people including our class president, and the president of SUNY at Buffalo, Bill Greiner and his wife, the former Carol Morrissey.

Tomie, who got what turned out to be his professional start as art editor of the Meriden High School *Annual* for 1952, which I had co-edited with Arthur von Au, had grown up as my wife's sole playmate in their neighborhood. He is currently engaged in writing his early autobiography in a set of serial children's "chapter books" in which Jean sometimes appears as a character. For a while in high school it had been a tossup whether Tomie would be an artist or a show business personality, and Carol had been Tomie's dance partner back then. Tomie was the first member of our class to be elected to the Meriden Hall of Fame, and Bill Greiner had been the third, on my nomination. I had been the second:

One day late in May of 1993 I got home to find that there were some messages on the phone, including one from Antonio Parisi in Connecticut who asked me to call him back because he had some good news for me — in the background his wife Tata could be heard on the tape saying, "Tell him what it's about," and Tony replied, "He'll call me back."

Tony Parisi had been my wife's and my music instructor at Meriden High School in the late 1940's and early 1950's. Jean had sung for him as a soprano in the Special Chorus of which I, too, had been a member. I'd sung, as well, in the Men's Glee Club, the Men's Octet, and I had been the lead singer in The Sportlanders barbershop quartet. Tony had sent Jean and me to the All-State Chorus, and I had gone as well to the All-New England Chorus one year, held in Lewiston-Auburn, Maine. We both sang in Tony's 1951 production of Gilbert and Sullivan's operetta, "H. M. S. Pinafore." In those days I was as heavily involved with singing as I was with writing and publishing my poems, articles, and stories in the local papers, the *Morning Record* and *The Journal* (later merged to become *The Record-Journal*). We dedicated the 1952 *Annual* to Tony.

When I called him back Tony informed me that I'd been elected to The Meriden Hall of Fame on the first ballot — unusual, he said, for someone to be elected on the first try. He told me that he had nominated me, that I'd be hearing from the chairperson shortly, and that the ceremony would be on a Sunday in October.

Flattered and delighted, I thanked Tony for his nomination. I asked where the Hall is located, and he said, "The old Curtis Memorial Library," which is a beautiful building made all of white marble outside with inlaid glass cubes for floors — a veritable Roman temple at the corner of East Main and Pleasant Streets. I used to love to go into the building when I was a kid, quite often after classes at Meriden High, which was on Pleasant Street just around the corner.

The Sunday before Halloween, as part of a reading tour, I drove to Meriden, and the next evening I gave a talk/reading at the Wallingford Public Library to a good crowd comprised of many friends and classmates, including Jim and Betty Masterson; Judge John Papandrea and his wife; the Fred Parisis — he had been my Sunday School teacher at the First Italian Baptist Church; Marie Delemarre Ho, whose birthday I shared; my nephew, John Knell, Anne, John's mother; Curtis Disbrow, his stepfather, and several others. My brother Gene and his wife, Judy, whom I had taken out to dinner at the Neptune House before the reading, were there too.

On Wednesday, the 27th, at the Meriden Public Library, I entertained an even larger crowd during a brown-bag literary luncheon. The Fred Parisis were there again, as were Sam and Marjorie Zavaglia from my dad's church, together with various other parishioners whom I vaguely recalled, and most of the Meriden Poetry Society. Again the Mastersons and Papandreas were present, as were Tony and Tata Parisi.

Warren and Julia Gardner arrived late and had to leave early to keep a doctor's appointment for Julia. Warren had been my boss at the *Morning Record* when I worked there while attending high school, and I imagine he'd had something to do with the two scholarships I'd received from the paper to attend the University of Connecticut after my discharge from the Navy in 1956.

I met Lynne Turdin at the luncheon — she had succeeded Lydia Atkinson as editor of the "Pennons of Pegasus" poetry column in the *Record-Journal* where I used to publish my young poems. Lynn tripled as the morgue clerk of the paper (one of my jobs back in the early 'fifties) and as historian of the Grace Baptist, which is what my father's church had become.

Marjorie Zavaglia, one of the main contributors to Turdin's column, kept interrupting my somewhat extemporaneous reminiscence / reading (I read Meriden poems and interspersed them with off-the-cuff comments) with tales of what I had been like when I was a kid. Afterward I chatted with people for a few minutes, including Win Carey, the wife of my old friend Walter, with whom I had collaborated on our class song in 1952, and Ruth Gendron, another classmate. Then Jim Masterson took me to lunch at the country club.

Jean came down on Saturday. She took the train but missed her connection in Springfield (it pulled away as the passengers from her late train struggled across the tracks toward it), so I drove up through terrible rain to fetch her. On Sunday morning Jean, Gene, Judy, my nephew Steve and his betrothed, Christine, attended Rev. Don Valentine's services at Grace Baptist. The parishioners did a huge reminiscence during the service itself. I read two poems about my parents, "May" and "Luigi" from *The Sketches,* and Lynn did a historical review of my dad's era and of my career in Meriden. The printed program was a souvenir issue.

Afterward there was a tea during which people testified about the many good things my parents had done for them. Lynn had prepared a large bulletin-board full of clippings from the papers, and she had a table full of scrapbooks that I didn't get a chance to look at because parishioners kept me busy talking and eating and reminiscing.

At two p.m. the induction into the Meriden Hall of Fame took place. There were three other inductees, one of whom was no longer living — a judge, an anthropologist, the late George Murdock, and me. Donald Dorsey, the judge, went on at great length, but my acceptance speech was a rather brief poem, "A Family Celebration." The audience was absolutely still as I read. Afterward many people came up to talk to me and tell me how much they'd liked it, including Dorsey. The day I was installed in the Meriden Hall of Fame was without a doubt the most gratifying day of my life.

But the 50th Anniversary Class Reunion made a near approach. The noon following the Pizza Party we had lunch at a nice restaurant, and then at 1:30 Jean went back to rest at the Ramada. I went with Marie and Alice out to my boyhood friend Pierre Bennerup's house in Berlin because his daughter, Brooke, wanted to meet me. I gave her a copy of my latest book of poems, *The Green Maces of Autumn, Voices in an Old Maine House.*

That evening I drove the original vanful plus Tomie to the Reunion itself at the Aqua Turf in Southington, and the place, though huge, was hopping with all sorts of gatherings including a wedding or two. The reunion had about 240 people in attendance including ninety-one year-old George Magrath, our Principal and later Superintendent of Schools, who was escorting the widow Tata Parisi. I got her to inscribe Jean's copy of *The Annual,* which we had brought along mainly for the purpose of identifying some of the unrecognizable old people who were wandering around.

I worked the room while Jean sat in one place and let people come to her. I chatted with Deedee Goodman and the Kreusberger twins, my classmates in the fifth and sixth grades at Benjamin Franklin School; Phil Reilly, from North Third Street; a bunch of people from Lincoln Junior High; the Honorable John Papandrea and many others that I'd known from all over the city.

Christopher showed up that night and stayed on the same floor with us at the Ramada. In the morning Jean and I had breakfast with Anne and Curt at Friendly's down the street, and then went to another Reunion event, a breakfast at the old Curtis Memorial, newly renovated as a civic center. Before its renovation it had housed the Meriden Hall of Fame, the original posthumous inductee of which was the immortal diva Rosa Ponselle whose father's establishment, Ponzillo's Tavern, was located almost across the street from the First Italian Baptist, which stuck in my father's craw.

My brother Gene had arranged a second Turco Family Reunion in the afternoon at the home of my nephew Stephen in Hebron. Like the previous year's reunion, it was stiflingly hot. Nevertheless, Jessie and little Jack drove around and around the house in a battery-powered miniature Jeep, and in the evening she didn't want to leave to drive back to Maine.

VIA FOLIOS

A refereed book series dedicated to Italian studies and the culture of Italian Americans in North America.

Most Recent Titles

PAOLINO ACCOLLA & NICCOLÒ D'AQUINO
Italici: An Encounter w/ Bassetti
Vol. 55, Italian Studies, $8.00

GIOSE RIMANELLI
The Three-Legged One
Vol. 54, Fiction, $15.00

CHARLES KLOPP, ED.
Bele Antiche Stòrie
Vol. 53, Italian Cultural Studies, $25.00

JOSEPH RICAPITO
Second Wave
Vol. 52, Poetry, $12.00

GARY MORMINO
Italians in Florida
Vol. 51, History, $15.00

GIANFRANCO ANGELUCCI
Federico F.
Vol. 50, Fiction, $16.00

ANTHONY VALERIO
The Little Sailor
Vol. 49, Memoir, $9.00

ROSS TALARICO
The Reptilian Interludes
Vol. 48, Poetry, $15.00

RACHEL GUIDO DEVRIES
Teeny Tiny Tino
Vol. 47, Children's Lit., $6.00

EMANUEL DIPASQUALE
Writing Anew
Vol. 46, Poetry, $15.00

Other VIA FOLIOS *Titles*

ADKINS, ET.AL, BRENT: ***SHIFTING BORDERS***; VOL. 42, CULTURAL CRITICISM, $18.00
BAROLINI, HELEN: ***Chiaroscuro: Essays of Identity***; Vol. 11, Essays, $15.00
BAROLINI, HELEN: ***More Italian Hours & Other Stories***; Vol. 28, Fiction, $16.00
BELLUSCIO, STEVEN: ***Constructing a Bibliography***; Vol. 37, Italian Americana, $15.00
BRIZIO-SKOV, ED., FLAVIA: ***Reconstructing Societies in the Aftermath of War***; Vol. 34, History/Cultural Studies, $30.00
CANNISTRARO, PHILIP: ***Blackshirts***; Vol. 17, History, $12.00
CARNEVALI, EMANUEL W/ DENNIS BARONE, ED. & AFTERWORD: ***FURNISHED ROOMS***; VOL. 43, POETRY, $14.00
CASEY, ET. AL, JOHN: ***Imagining Humanity***; Vol. 25, Interdisciplinary Studies, $18.00
CLEMENTS, ARTHUR L. ***The Book of Madness and Love***; Vol. 26, Poetry, $10.00
CONDINI, NED: ***Quartettsatz***; Vol. 7, Poetry, $7.00

CORSI, JONE GAILLARD: ***Il libretto d'autore, 1860–1930***; Vol. 12, Criticism, $17.00
FAMÀ, MARIA: ***LOOKING FOR COVER***; VOL. 45, POETRY, $15.00; CD, $6.00
FEINSTEIN, WILEY: ***Humility's Deceit: Calvino Reading Ariosto Reading Calvino***; Vol. 3, Criticism, $10.00
GARDAPHÈ, FRED L. ***Moustache Pete is Dead!*** Vol. 13, Oral literature, $10.00
GARDAPHÉ, FRED, PAOLO GIORDANO, AND ANTHONY JULIAN TAMBURRI: ***INTRODUCING ITALIAN AMERICANA: GENERALITIES ON LITERATURE AND FILM***; VOL. 40, CRITICISM $10.00
GIORDANO, ED., PAOLO A. ***Joseph Tusiani: Poet, Translator, Humanist***; Vol. 2, Criticism, $25.00
GIOSEFFI, DANIELA: ***Blood Autumn / Autunno di sangue***; Vol. 39, Poetry, $15.00/$25.00
GIOSEFFI, DANIELA: ***Going On***; Vol. 23, Poetry, $10.00
GIOSEFFI, DANIELA: ***Word Wounds and Water Flowers***; Vol. 4, Poetry, $8.00
GRAMSCI, ANTONIO; TRANS. AND INTROD. BY PAOLO VERDICCHIO: ***The Southern Question***; Vol. 5, Social Criticism, $5.00
GUIDA, GEORGE: ***LOW ITALIAN***;VOL. 41, POETRY, $11.00
HOSTERT, ANNA CAMAITI, and ANTHONY JULIAN TAMBURRI, EDS. ***Screening Ethnicity***; Vol. 30, Ital. Amer. Culture, $25.00
LAGIER, JENNIFER: ***Second Class Citizen***; Vol. 19, Poetry, $8.00
LIMA, ROBERT: ***Sardinia • Sardegna***; Vol. 24, Poetry, $10.00
MESSINA, ED., ELIZABETH GIOVANNA: ***In Our Own Voices***; Vol. 32, Italian American Studies, $25.00
MISURELLA, FRED: ***Lies to Live by***; Vol. 38, Stories, $15.00
MISURELLA, FRED: ***Short Time***; Vol. 8, Novella, $7.00
NASI, ED., FRANCO: ***Intorno alla Via Emilia***; Vol. 27, Culture, $16.00
PARATI, GABRIELLA, and BEN LAWTON, EDS. ***Italian Cultural Studies***; Vol. 29, Essays, $18.00
PASQUALE, EMANUEL DI: ***The Silver Lake Love Poems***; Vol. 21, Poetry, $7.00
PICARAZZI, TERESA, and WILEY FEINSTEIN, EDS. ***An African Harlequin in Milan***; Vol. 10, Theater/Essays, $15.00
PUGLIESE, STANISLAO G. ***Desperate Inscriptions***; Vol. 31, History, $12.00
RICAPITO, JOSEPH: ***Florentine Streets and Other Poems***; Vol. 9, Poetry, $9.00
RUSTICHELLI, ED., LUIGI: ***Seminario sul racconto***; Vol. 16, Narrativa, $10.00
RUSTICHELLI, ED., LUIGI: ***Seminario sulla drammaturgia***; Vol. 14, Theater/Essays, $10.00
STEFANILE, FELIX: ***The Country of Absence***; Vol. 18, Poetry, $9.00
TALARICO, ROSS: ***The Journey Home***; Vol. 22, Poetry, $12.00
TAMBURRI, ED. ET. AL, ANTHONY JULIAN ***Italian Cultural Studies 2001***; Vol. 33, Essays, $18.00
TAMBURRI, ED., ANTHONY JULIAN with MARY JO BONA, INTROD. ***Fuori: Essays by Italian/American Lesbians and Gay***; Vol. 6, Essays, $10.00
TAMBURRI, ED., ANTHONY JULIAN: ***Italian Cultural Studies 2002***; Vol. 36, Essays, $18.00
TURCO, LEWIS: ***Shaking the Family Tree***; Vol. 15, Poetry, $9.00
TUSIANI, BEA: ***con amore***; Vol. 35, Memoir, $19.00
TUSIANI, JOSEPH: ***Ethnicity***; Vol. 20, Selected Poetry, $12.00
VALERIO, ANTHONY: ***TONY CADE BAMBARA'S ONE SICILIAN NIGHT***; VOL. 44, MEMOIR, $10.00
VISCUSI, ROBERT: ***Oration Upon the Most Recent Death of Christopher Columbus***; Vol. 1, Poetry, $3.00

Published by BORDIGHERA, INC., an independently owned not-for-profit scholarly organization that has no legal affiliation to the University of Central Florida or John D. Calandra Italian American Institute, Queens College/CUNY.